REAL FOOD REAL SIMPLE

80+ PLANT-BASED RECIPES TO SATISFY YOUR SOUL

BY: HANNAH JANISH

REAL FOOD REAL SIMPLE

ISBN#978-1-949950-53-3

CONTENTS

CONTENTS

CONTENTS

QUICK BITES

COMFORT FOODS

CONTENTS

EPIC DINNERS

SWEET TREATS

RESOURCES

WELCOME

W hether your goal is to look more vibrant and youthful, regain your health or lose weight for good, this recipe book will give you plenty of mouth watering recipes that will leave you feeling satiated but also eager to live life. We didn't stop there though. We have included a number of simple tips for looking and feeling your best.

Starches and fruits on their own can be a little bland but through the amazing photos and recipes contained in Real Food Real Simple, I hope to inspire you to introduce more of these healthy satisfying meals in to your life. These are my favorite recipes and I hope they become staples in your life.

WHOLE FOODS

One of the primary focuses of the Lean & Clean movement and my recipe books is to promote the consumption of more whole foods. You know... foods that don't have an ingredient list. The foods that are the ingredients.

The reason why I promote more whole foods is simple - they are far more nutritious and satisfying to our bodies. Refined and processed foods are deficient in fibre, phytonutrients, vitamins and minerals. It's these components of the food that makes it healthy but through the refinement process, we strip these vital components.

Why are whole foods important for weight loss? Whole foods are satisfying. They provide us with the fibre, phytonutrients, vitamins and minerals that our bodies require. A major reason why people eating a standard American diet are overweight is because the foods they eat are so processed that they are deficient in vitamins and minerals. The body is still starving for these vital components of health, so they reach for more and more food. Their bodies become overfed but undernourished. It is this overconsumption of highly processed carbohydrates and refined fats that end up on their waist lines.

WELCOME

The majority of the recipes in Real Food Real Simple use only whole foods. While we do use some processed ingredients, I do so sparingly to give you options and to improve your relationship with food. For example the 'Pumpkin Muffins' in this book do use whole wheat flour which isn't a whole food but is a far healthier muffin then something you will buy in your local grocery store which will be laden with oils or animal products.

The idea isn't to completely banish processed ingredients for the rest of our lives but to make a slow transition to eating more whole food meals. This gives you a much healthier relationship with food, relaxes your mindset and you learn to trust your body with finding it's natural weight.

INTUITIVE EATING

Remember when you were a kid and you never thought about food? Why would you right? You were way too busy enjoying your life, playing outside, laughing and learning all the time than to worry about salt, fat, calories and how much water you consume on a daily basis. What a life! What happened to that?

The farther that we get away from the diet we were biologically adapted to eat, the more problems we have. We see so many people in the high carb vegan community completely stressed out on what to eat, when to eat, where to eat and literally dissecting every single little thing they do when it comes to what they put in their mouth, but the truth is, you are the last person that needs to worry about what you eat. A high carb vegan diet is the healthiest diet you can eat. It is the easiest way to lose weight, look younger and feel amazing.

SO WHAT IS THE PROBLEM HERE?

We've become so disconnected from that child inside of us, the one that we used to be, that just let everything flow, enjoyed life as it came at us, ate when we were hungry and stopped when our body told us to stop. We have no idea how much to eat anymore. We use food more like a drug, we find peace, love and comfort in the act of eating instead of using it for what it is, energy and nourishment for our bodies.

The biggest thing when it comes to intuitive eating is eating the right foods, that means a high carb, low fat, starch-centred diet is going to give your body everything it needs. We've got that one covered!

Second. Throw everything you've ever learned about calories and how much to eat out the window. Got it? Good.

Intuitive eating, like I said above. Is learning to eat when you are truly hungry and stopping when you are satiated. We've become so detached from this, especially when we grow up our entire lives eating processed, overly stimulating, high fat, high salt, high sugar foods. These foods can actually act as a drug in our system and hijack our brains to get us to eat way beyond what we would ever need or even want to eat. The worst thing is when we switch to a healthy diet comprised of whole foods this habit can follow us and completely hamper your results if you have an addiction to food. So in reality, eating intuitively is really just a fancy word for 'eating'.

You know what we did as a child and before we found out about calorie restriction? Just eat when you're hungry till you're full. If you have food left on your plate or in your bowl and you are no longer attracted or wanting to eat that food, then you're done. You can come back to it later or just save it for the next meal. If you find that you are hungry in an hour, then eat.

Eating intuitively is not about deprivation or restriction. It is about finding that sweet spot. Where you eat until you feel satiated but haven't eaten so much that you want to vomit or go to sleep. It takes time and practice but over time it becomes so much easier and really enjoyable.

All of the popular high carb plant-based doctors (Dr. McDougall, Dr. Esselstyn, T. Colin Campbell, Dr. Greger, Dr. Barnard,

John Robbins, etc) recommend eating intuitively. None of them recommend eating a certain caloric number or restricting. We like to follow the advice of these pioneers as they have helped tens of thousands regain their health and lose the weight for good.

HOW MANY CALORIES SHOULD I EAT?

This is the million dollar question that everyone seems to want to know and the honest truth is... I don't know.

The reason why I don't know is because you are a unique and wonderful being. Your health history, muscle to fat ratio, activity levels, height and weight are all different. Giving a specific calorie recommendation is very difficult based on all of these factors.

What I do recommend for weight loss and health is to eat until you are satiated. That doesn't mean to calorie restrict or to stuff your face to the point of wanting to vomit. That means, when you've eaten enough, you know you have because you feel satisfied with how much you've eaten. You are no longer eager or excited to eat your food anymore. If you're hungry in a hour after you finish your meal, feel free to eat some more.

The Lean & Clean lifestyle is not about deprivation, it is about feeling full and satisfied. It is not a diet fad that you will do for next 30 days and expect to lose 30lbs.

It is a lifestyle that promotes long-term health by supplying your body with ample healthy calories so that you can really live your life, regain your health and lose the weight for good.

SELF-LOVE

Another pillar of the Lean & Clean lifestyle and this recipe book is self-love. Recognizing the magnificent beings that we already are, is a beautiful thing. Like anything in the world, deeply loving ourselves is a practice much like meditation. Something that we work at on a daily basis but are the cards stacked in our favor?

We live in a world that bombards us with nifty marketing that picks at our insecurities and promises that if we just buy their fancy product, we will feel better about ourselves. Does this actually happen? Is our self-worth dependant on the latest fashion or looking like the model in that ad? Absolutely not but a lot of us have been trapped in a cycle where we are solely focusing on the external. Do I look good enough? Are my clothes good enough? Will they like me?

What is the difference between the people who are fully deeply in love with themselves versus those that are not? Were they born with some innate talent of self-love? Do they have more money in the bank? Do they have six pack abs? You may find yourself chuckling at these statements but a lot of you, including me, believe this to some degree.

The difference lies in how they are thinking about themselves the majority of the time. Instead of picking away at all the imperfections that they hate about themselves, they choose to embrace their own uniqueness and relish in the fact that they are a perfectly imperfect being and that… is reason to celebrate.

Mastering the mind comes down to choosing. Choosing to feel love for yourself. Making that choice over and over again. Maybe you make that choice 100 times during each day and each time you make that choice, you are training your mind to think those thoughts. You are creating a groove out of rock and at first you have a small stream trickling through but over time with more choices, you have a river flowing abundantly.

How do you choose to feel love for yourself? It's quite simple actually. Repeat the phrase "I love myself." Say it to yourself right now. Say it 10 times in your mind. You can't help but have a small smile on your face :).

By making the choice of repeating this mantra in your mind, you are choosing to love yourself and therefore replacing those negative thoughts in your mind with positive loving ones.

Ask yourself the question, "If I loved myself truly and deeply, how would I feel right now?" Would you feel love, peace, joy, excitement, inspiration or gratitude? Of course you would! You would be feeling all of those great things right now. Anytime you may be feeling down or not as good as you'd like, ask yourself that question and think of all those emotions that you would be feeling. I guarantee that you will feel better instantly and by feeling better in this moment, you are choosing love for yourself.

There may be times when you are in a very negative thought loop. The first thing to do is to recognize that it is in fact just a thought loop. Those thoughts aren't you. You are the awareness behind the thought. Then ask yourself another question, "is this thought loop useful?" Just by asking yourself that and recognizing what is going on, brings awareness and presence. Then you can move towards more positive and loving thoughts by repeating your new self-love mantra.

I think that self-love is such an important part of living our lives to the fullest and it is another pillar of having an abundant life. I recommend that you check out the book "Love Yourself Like Your Life Depends On It" by Kamal Ravikant. The book costs just a few dollars on Amazon and is a great accessory to this recipe book. It is a very simple yet effective approach to self-love.

Remember, loving yourself is a state of mind, a state of feeling great. You have the power and the choice to feel it right now.

FITNESS TIPS

Eating a plant-based whole foods diet will provide great results on it's own and account for approximately 80% of your weight loss goals. I do recommend that an important part of any healthy lifestyle is the inclusion of fitness and exercise. I think you will find my recommendations to be both easy, fun and simple to include in to your current life.

When it comes to building and increasing our fitness, it can be much simpler than what you may think. While there are many ways that you can go about exercising your body such as HIIT, hiring a personal trainer or going to group classes at a local gym, I don't recommend them for most people. The reason for that is they can be expensive, too difficult for your current fitness level or hard on your ligaments and tendons. You may want to try these in the future or right now. As always, it is entirely up to you.

The Lean & Clean lifestyle is about having a healthy relationship with food and we want to extend that relationship to exercise as well. I want you to focus on gentle exercises that will be easy on your body. If you try to do exercises that are too difficult for you right now, you could end up easily injuring yourself. The two activities that we recommend for weight loss and building fitness is brisk walking and cycling. Both of these exercises are both very gentle on the body, can be done by almost anyone and are inexpensive to participate in.

I suggest setting aside 1 hour to do a fitness session. 1 hour gives you time to do a proper warm up, max effort and cool down. These are all important parts of a session so that you reduce the risk of injury and can stay consistent over the long term. I recommend spending between 2-3 hours per week building your fitness. Maybe you'll be able to do more but that is a good baseline to start.

The three components I mentioned above is the warm up, max effort and cool down. Let's discuss what each one means and its purpose.

A warm up is the time that you spend walking or cycling at an easy pace. A pace that it is easy for you to talk, your breathing is light and comfortable for you to do. During this time your heart rate will be typically around 105-130 beats per minute. This is also known as the fat burning or recovery zone. Not only is it important for fat burning to be in this zone but it warms up your muscles for the max effort you will be doing next.

The max effort is when you will be pushing your body to a level that might not be entirely comfortable for you. Don't worry, this is for a short period of time. You will experience muscle fatigue and heavy breathing. During this time your heart rate will typically be between 150-180 beats per minute. This zone will really build your fitness level. Something I see often is that people will do a lot of exercise but they will never really push their body. Consistently pushing your body will improve your fitness level and help you accelerate your results.

The cool down is the time when you will be recovering from the max effort. You will be walking or cycling at a very comfortable pace. Heart rate again will be between 105-130 beats per minute. The purpose of the cool down is to let your body recover and give time for your heart rate to lower back to normal. If you really pushed yourself, the cool down can be a time where you experience a rush of feel good endorphins from working so hard in the max effort!

With understanding the basics of a workout, let's put it all together based on a 1 hour work out interval.

Warm up   30-35 minutes
Max effort   3-5 minutes
Cool down   20-25 minutes

Now the easiest way to perform a 'max effort' is by either cycling up a hill or walking up steps or a hill. When you take your body vertically up, it will be very stressful and raise your heart rate to a level where you are not comfortable. So with this in mind, think about exactly where you will be able to do this in your location. If there aren't any hills, you can still do a max effort while cycling on flat land. Walking would be more difficult to do so since if you were to push yourself, it might turn in to a jog or run.

If for example, it takes you only about 1 minute to ride up a hill that you are using for your max effort, you can do laps of that hill. So ride to the top, ride down, ride up, ride down, ride up, ride down. So that way you still have approximately 3 minutes of max effort.

Now, if you are a novice with regards to fitness and quite overweight, you may want to skip the max effort all together and just focus on keeping a brisk pace while walking or cycling. As you lose weight, it will be easier in the future to push your body. If you do choose to do max efforts consistently, only spend 3-10 minutes per week in that zone.

WELCOME

Building your fitness by yourself can be a bit boring at times. Why not find a friend or family member that you can exercise with. You could even join a local cycling/hiking/walking club (check Facebook and Meetup). If you make exercise a social event, it will be so much more fun to do and will hold you accountable as well. Also if you exercise with people that are fitter than you, it will help push you to the next level effortlessly. If you prefer to exercise by yourself due to logistics or personal preference, listen to some excellent audiobooks while on your walks or bike rides!

Make sure you are properly hydrated as well. Drink 0.5-1 quarts (litres) of water before your exercise session and bring a small bottle with you to sip on. Try not to eat within 1 hour of starting your work out so that your food has time to digest.

Just remember that the majority of results will come from your food choices. Incorporating exercise and fitness in to your life is a part of a healthy lifestyle. Keep it simple, fun and comfortable!

MY THOUGHTS ON SALT

A lot of people in the high carb community say that you cannot lose weight if you consume too much salt. I have found through my own experimentation for this to be completely false. So far, I have lost 70lbs without even paying any attention to my sodium intake. But recently with all the talk about salt, I did an experiment of drastically reducing our sodium down to less than 500 mg per day (just to see what happens) and I ended up losing around 10lbs of water weight. Now this weight is not fat! It is water and it will come back by introducing the amount of sodium we used to consume. So what's the lesson here? Our bodies will hold excess water the more sodium that we eat but we can easily drop (and regain) this weight by manipulating the amount of sodium we consume on a daily basis.

What else? Well salt is very delicious on our foods and I do think that while salt intake may not effect your health in a negative way, I do actually believe it can drive you to eat more than you really need. Why? Because like I said - salt is delicious! One of the biggest things that I promote is intuitive eating. Which basically means eating until your food no longer tastes as good as it did when you first started eating. Now this can be very hard to do if you put a ton of flavor enhancers on your food, like salt. If you are practicing intuitive eating you will want to cut out the salt, for the time being, until you are more in tune with your body and what it really needs.

Much of the bad press that salt gets is that it raises blood pressure. This information is from outdated research where the studies concluded that reducing sodium intake to less than 500mg daily, which is a drastic change from the 2,300mg daily USDA guideline, will reduce your blood pressure. Has this recommendation worked? No. A low-sodium diet is not palatable for most people. Salt makes, otherwise bland food, much more enjoyable to eat.

Sodium gets a very bad rap since it is consistently mixed with animal foods that are high in saturated fats and cholesterol. These animal foods build up plaque in the arteries and therefore raising blood pressure.

Dr. McDougall states in the Starch Solution that participants at his 10-day live-in programs noticed an average reduction for people with a starting blood pressure (140/90 mmHg or greater) is 15 points systolic and 13 points diastolic in 7 days. These people also stopped taking their blood pressure medication when beginning his program. When compared with randomized clinical trials where participants were eating the SAD diet, they reduced their sodium intake on average by 1,725mg so they were consuming the USDA guideline of 2,300mg daily, and only noticed a reduction of 1 to 5 points systolic and 0.6 to 3 points diastolic.

I recommend doing your own experiment with salt and find what works best for you! Also if you are to add salt to your food, do so after it has already been cooked. If you add it in while it is cooking, the taste is dissipated.

I would also recommend measuring it out so that you really know how much you are adding in.

1/8 tsp	250 mg
1/4 tsp	575 mg
1/2 tsp	1150 mg
1 tsp	2325 mg
1 tbsp	6976 mg

THE TRUTH ABOUT GLUTEN

More and more grocery and health food stores stock gluten-free products. That's good news for people with celiac disease, who for health reasons should not eat wheat with gluten. But most of the people who reach for gluten-free products do not have celiac disease and or even a sensitivity to wheat.

Many people may just perceive that a gluten-free diet is healthier when in reality, it is basically just a more expensive, higher in fat and 'doesn't taste as great' kind of diet, that is if you're buying all the fancy "GF" products. The term "Gluten-Free" has really just become a craze. Why? Marketing. Because it is marketed so well, people have made it into this magic pill for health and weight loss, just like they did with sugar-free, fat-free, and everything else "free" that they can make you "believe" is better for you and sell you of course. Avoiding gluten isn't going to do much for your health except make you worry every time you go out for Italian food and we can see this in cultures that have thrived off of wheat for tens of thousands of years like the Egyptians and Middle Eastern civilizations.

Gluten is completely harmless unless you have celiac disease. Dr. Greger puts this in to a great perspective when he says "Just because some people have a peanut allergy, doesn't mean everyone should avoid peanuts," but for people with celiac disease, a gluten-free diet is essential. So what is celiac disease?

Celiac disease is a condition, caused by an abnormal immune response to gluten, which can damage the lining of the small intestine. That, in turn, can prevent important nutrients from being absorbed into the body and cause major deficiencies. Symptoms of celiac disease include diarrhea, anemia, bone pain, and a severe skin rash called dermatitis herpetiformis. If you believe you have a sensitivity or allergy to gluten you will need to go to your doctor to be properly tested.

For the 98% of the population that does not have celiac disease, whole grains are actually health promoting. Whole grains are rich in many components including: dietary fibre, starch, antioxidant nutrients, minerals, vitamins, lignans and phenolic compounds that have been linked to the reduced risk of coronary heart disease, cancer, obesity and other chronic diseases. In fact, eating a gluten-free diet when you do not have celiac disease can lead to these nutritional deficiencies especially if you are replacing whole grains with their gluten-free counterparts.

In this book you can choose whichever type of flour, pasta, or grain you want to use in each recipe. For baked items we specifically put 1 cup of flour so that you can substitute brown rice, whole wheat, corn or whatever type of flour you like the best. They are all interchangeable. The same thing goes for pasta. If the recipe says 8 ounces of cappellini, you can use whichever kind you like. I wanted to mention gluten and the common fears about it because it is completely unnecessary to avoid it if you don't have to.

As always I preach a diet of whole foods and believe that is best for maximum weight loss and health so definitely do not go centering your diet around muffins and pasta, regardless of what kind of flour it's made out of. These are fine to eat moderately but make sure you are eating the bulk of your diet from whole foods like potatoes, rice, corn, beans and as always keep it low fat and high carb.

TRACKING YOUR PROGRESS

For many people, weight loss is an important reason for joining the Lean & Clean lifestyle and tracking your progress through photos is a great way to do it. It will give a great visual chronology of your transformation.

I don't recommend using a scale to track your progress. Your weight can fluctuate so much throughout the day and through the week based on your hydration levels as well as how much food you've eaten.

If you showcase your transformation photos on instagram, make sure you tag @highcarbhannah so that I can see them.

If you feel comfortable doing so, you can submit your transformation photos to hannah@highcarbhannah.co. I would love to share them on my social media accounts to promote more health, love and well-being.

Here are some tips to ensure you are taking great photos throughout your transformation.

1. Take your before photos prior to practicing the principles in Real Food Real Simple

2. Assume a natural stance, no flexing or posing!

3. Take both one front view and one side view photo.

4. Keep all the photos that you take, no deleting any of them

5. Set a reminder on your phone to take photos every 4 weeks

6. Wear a bra or crop top with underwear or shorts.

7. Take the photos in the same place using the same mirror

8. Take the photo on the same level, vertically and horizontally

9. Make sure your photos are full length shots of your body

10. Take the photo at the same time of day (i.e. just after you wake up)

11. Keep your feet together and ankles touching

12. Keep the camera away from your face

SOCIAL DIFFICULTIES OF BEING PLANT BASED

You know what's interesting? What I have found to be the most difficult part of eating a plant-based diet is the social aspect of it. Whether you're a cooked vegan, raw vegan or somewhere in between, the people around you sometimes just find it so weird that you no longer eat animal products. They may ask you about your eating habits.

"So wait... you don't eat meat or drink milk... surely you must eat cheese... no cheese? Surely you must eat fish, everyone eats fish... no fish? Well how do you get your protein?"

That is the type of conversation that you could have when you explain to someone that you no longer eat any animal products. People are really curious about you because it's seems so far out of their reality that you don't eat meat, dairy or eggs anymore. After they enquire about every little bit of your food intake, they will typically follow up with something like this. "Well I don't eat THAT much meat, just a little bit... but cheese, I love cheese, I could never give it up."

If you've been eating a plant-based diet for some time, you'll probably chuckle at this because this is almost always how these conversations go. It starts with someone asking you many questions then following up with a justification for how they live their life.

Now I don't think people who are eating animal products are bad people at all but isn't it funny that many people who do eat animal products will justify their eating habits in some type of way to you. It's almost as if they know on some level that what they are doing isn't necessarily the best for them and that it is causing harm to other beings.

For the majority of people who are eating animal products they are doing so out of ignorance. No, they aren't being rude, it's just that they aren't necessarily educated on the science and facts surrounding animal products and how it can be detrimental to their health, the environment and the animals.

As well as being ignorant of the ramifications of their food choices, they are doing so because it is a deeply engrained habit. It is something that almost all of us grow up with. There are few people in the world that grow up completely plant-based, those few lucky ones.

With this understanding, when people challenge you about eating a plant-based diet with jokes or rude remarks, you must realize that this is not a reflection of you and how you are living. It is a reflection of them and how they feel about themselves and their life. There is nothing wrong with that and we should never condemn or make others feel inferior about this.

Understand that when you tell someone you're plant-based or vegan, it's a statement in and of itself. That statement rings loud and clear in their ears and it is almost confrontational at times. Derek, my husband, has had someone in the grocery store make a rather rude comment. He was loading up my rice and veggies on to the converyor and the gentleman infront of him asked if the tattoo on my finger, which says "Vegan", was real or fake. He told him that it was real and the gentleman responded with, "I would've respected you a lot more if it was fake."

At first, he was totally shocked. He was not expecting that at all. Later Derek understood that his dietary choices was challenging others beliefs. The foods the gentleman was paying for were pop and chips which made sense to Derek. He didn't look like a particularly healthy fellow but should Derek let his comments affect how he lives? Of course not.

One of the main reasons I believe that people make a lot of these rude comments about being plant-based is because they want you to conform to their reality. They want you to change back to eating animal products and unhealthy foods because if you were to resume your prior eating habits, it would make them feel better about their poor choices.

If you're new to eating plant-based, you may have family members or friends that egg you on (sorry for the pun) to eat a little bit of their food. They may say, "Oh come on, have a hamburger... one hamburger won't hurt you!" This is pretty typical and to be expected. Stand your ground though, don't let the social pressure affect the choice that you've made for the health of your body, the animals and the planet.

WELCOME

It can sometimes be difficult to say no in those circumstances but as you do it more often, the easier it becomes. It is also important to plan ahead. If you're going to a family gathering or to a friend's place to eat, it is usually best to assume that they don't know what you can and cannot eat. This means that supplying your own food in these circumstances might be the best thing to do. While this may seem a little weird at first, it may take a lot of stress off the host because they may not have any idea of what to make for you. Some people, while they may not eat a plant-based diet are educated on the topic enough to know what you can and cannot eat.

Eating out at restaurants is another situation that can be difficult. Always try to choose vegan restaurants or restaurants that advertise that they have vegan options, www.happycow.net (they have an app too) is a great website to find these places). If you're going to a restaurant where you are unsure of the options that will be available to you, then have a meal at home before you get to the restaurant. As weird as this sounds, it can really save you from making a poor choice. If you've already eaten then it gives you more options to choose from. Instead of having to order an entrée, you can order a side salad and still be satisfied because you've eaten beforehand.

Another trick is when you are ordering from a menu that you are unsure of, let the waiter or waitress know that you are allergic to meat, dairy and eggs. They will relay that information back to the chef making your food and the last thing they want is to have an ambulance at their door step because a customer had an allergic reaction. Most restaurants are getting better and are offering more plant-based options as it becomes more popular.

If you don't have any plant-based or vegan friends, then make it a priority to meet these people in your area. It is so refreshing to speak with people who share this very important lifestyle with you. It's great because fellow vegans and plant-based eaters understand you. You have something in common and for most people being vegan is a very important part of their life.

With the growing network of people on facebook, youtube,

instagram and other social media platforms, it is becoming increasingly easy to meet up and make friends. Search for local vegan groups on facebook or checkout www.meetup.com for meetup groups in your area. It can make things much more enjoyable for your life to meet more like minded friends following the same lifestyle.

Another important topic that I think should be discussed more is about our significant others. A common story that I hear is that someone meets a great person, they both eat a standard American diet and one of them starts eating plant-based and that person wants their partner to also eat plant-based.

This can be a very tricky situation because you started a relationship together, you changed and then you want them to change to match how your life has changed. Now, this isn't necessarily fair to the other party involved because you are putting a condition on the relationship. You may think that if your partner was plant-based then you'd be happier or love them more. It is not good to think like this, especially if you do want your partner to change.

You must love your significant other no matter what. It must be unconditional because if they sense that you are putting conditions on your love for them because of their eating habits, it can cause resentment in the relationship. By showing your partner unconditional love, they feel better about themselves and from there you can educate them on the benefits from eating plant-based. Make sure they know that you love them no matter what they eat and this in turn can create the space they may need to make the transition. Live by being an example of health, positivity and love and those around you will become intrigued and follow your daring lead.

For those of you who are single and want to meet a vegan partner, then put out that wish to the universe. Write out the type of partner you desire in the form of a script. List out the qualities and traits that you love and think of all the emotions you would be feeling.

DEHYDRATING WITHOUT A DEHYDRATOR

Only a handful of the recipes in this book use a dehydrator but if you don't have one, don't worry there are still a few options that you have to dehydrate your food. Keep in mind that using an oven or toaster oven won't give you the same temperature control as an Excalibur dehydrator so your food may not be completely raw.

Option #1 - Use Your Oven

First, start your oven on the lowest possible setting. If your oven has a convection function, set that as well to keep the air flowing. You can use a regular fan pointed in to the oven to get the same effect. Place the foods you want to dehydrate on a pan with a non-stick sheet like parchment paper. Put the pan in the oven and keep the door of the oven cracked open and the fan blowing fresh air in.

Keep in mind that the time to dehydrate using an oven will probably be significantly less, so keep an eye on it.

Option #2 - Use Your Toaster Oven

Using your toaster oven is essentially going to be the same as in option one. Put the toaster oven on the lowest setting and if you can, setup a fan to keep the air circulating to avoid moisture buildup in the oven. Place the foods you want to dehydrate on a pan with a non-stick sheet like parchment paper. Put the pan in the toaster oven and keep the door of the toaster oven cracked open.

Again, the dehydrating time will probably be significantly less using this method.

JUICES & SMOOTHIES

⟶

PUMPKIN SMOOTHIE

SERVINGS	PREP TIME	COOK TIME
1	5 MINUTES	0 MINUTES

INGREDIENTS

1	cup canned pumpkin
1-2	frozen bananas
1	ripe persimmon
3-4	dates, pitted
1/2	tsp cinnamon
1/2	tsp ginger
1	cup water or coconut water

INSTRUCTIONS

To make the smoothie just throw all the ingredients in your blender on high and process till smooth.

If you don't have a Vitamix or Blendtec blender, you may need to let the frozen bananas thaw for 30 minutes beforehand so that it blends much more smoothly.

POWER SMOOTHIE

SERVINGS	PREP TIME	COOK TIME
1	5 MINUTES	0 MINUTES

INGREDIENTS

1/2   head romaine
1   cup spinach
1   mango or 1 cup frozen mango
1   cup water or coconut water
2-3   frozen bananas

INSTRUCTIONS

To make the smoothie just throw all the ingredients in your blender on high and process till smooth.

Another thing we love to do is chop up extra banana and mango and put it on top and eat it like a smoothie bowl.

It's also great with extra coconut flakes or mulberries on top. Get creative with it :)

CHUNKY MONKEY SMOOTHIE

SERVINGS	PREP TIME	COOK TIME
1	5 MINUTES	0 MINUTES

INGREDIENTS

3 frozen bananas

2 fresh ripe bananas

2 Medjool dates

2 tbsp powdered peanut butter

2 tbsp cacao powder

1/2 cup water

INSTRUCTIONS

Blend frozen bananas, water, cacao and powdered peanut butter in blender until there are no visible chunks.

Pour into mason jar.

Chop up bananas and dates and mix half of them into the base of the smoothie and use the rest to garnish.

You can also sprinkle a little extra peanut butter powder, coconut flakes or cacao nibs on top if you like.

MANGO ORANGE SMOOTHIE

SERVINGS	PREP TIME	COOK TIME
1	10 MINUTES	0 MINUTES

INGREDIENTS

4 cups fresh orange juice (about 10 fresh oranges)

2 cups frozen mango

1 ripe fresh mango

2 tbsp shredded coconut

INSTRUCTIONS

Juice your oranges and place in blender. Dump in your frozen mango and blend on high for 30 seconds or until there are no visible chunks.

Pour into mason jar.

Chop up fresh mango by scoring it first. Scoop out one half with a spoon and mix into the base of the smoothie.

Add the remaining mango chunks and coconut to top.

ARTISAN JUICES

SERVINGS	PREP TIME	COOK TIME
1	5 MINUTES	0 MINUTES

SUNRISE CLEANSER

3	large cucumbers
4	stalks celery
1/2	bunch lacinato kale
2	lemons, juiced

SPICY CARROT

4	carrots
2	apples
2	lemons, juiced
2-3	pieces turmeric root
1	inch of ginger

CLEAN GREEN

2	apples
2	large cucumbers
1/2	bunch cilantro
1/2	bunch lacinato kale
1	lemon, juiced
1/2	fennel bulb

INSTRUCTIONS

My husband Derek used to work at local raw organic juice company and these recipes are inspired by our favorite juice recipes from there.

ADD-INS

Some interesting things you can add in to juices are avocados and hemp protein powder.

To add avocado in to a juice, take about 1/4 or 1/8 of an avocado and blend it with a small amount of the juice you just made.

After you get a creamy juice mix, blend in the rest of the juice and enjoy. It sounds a little strange but try it out!

If using hemp protein, we recommend to blend it in when using avocado in your juice. Just follow the same instructions above and add in 1 tbsp of the protein powder.

COCONUT CHOCOLATE SMOOTHIE

SERVINGS	PREP TIME	COOK TIME
1	5 MINUTES	0 MINUTES

INGREDIENTS

3-5   frozen bananas

1   cup water or coconut water

2   tbsp cacao powder

1   fresh ripe banana

2   Medjool dates

2   tbsp coconut flakes

1   tbsp cacao nibs

INSTRUCTIONS

Blend frozen bananas, coconut water and cacao powder until there are no visible chunks.

Pour into jar.

Chop up the ripe banana and medjool dates and mix half into the base of the smoothie and use the other half to garnish the top along with the coconut flakes and cacao nibs.

LOADED MAQUI SMOOTHIE

SERVINGS	PREP TIME	COOK TIME
1	5 MINUTES	0 MINUTES

INGREDIENTS

3   frozen bananas

2   tbsp maqui powder

1/2   cup water

1   fresh ripe banana

1/2   cup frozen cherries

1/2   fresh ripe mango

1/2   cup fresh pineapple

2   tbsp coconut flakes

2   tbsp mulberries

INSTRUCTIONS

Blend frozen bananas, maqui powder and water until there are no visible chunks.

Pour into jar.

Chop up banana, mango, pineapple and mix into base of the smoothie along with the frozen berries and cherries.

Top with mulberries, coconut flakes and any other leftover fruit.

FRESH
START →

BANANA MANGO PUDDING

SERVINGS	PREP TIME	COOK TIME
1	5 MINUTES	0 MINUTES

INGREDIENTS

2   frozen bananas

1   ripe banana, chopped

3   mangoes

1   tbsp coconut flakes

1   cup water or coconut water

INSTRUCTIONS

Take 2 1/2 of your mangoes, reserving the other half, your frozen bananas and your coconut water or water and blend them on low in your blender until the mixture is smooth and creamy.

You may need to let the frozen bananas thaw for 15-30 minutes before blending.

Next take the reserved mango and chop into chunks.

Pour your pudding mixture into a large bowl, top with chopped banana, mango and coconut flakes.

RAW CEREAL

SERVINGS	PREP TIME	COOK TIME
1	5 MINUTES	0 MINUTES

MILK INGREDIENTS

2	frozen bananas
1/4	tsp vanilla extract
1	tsp cinnamon
1	cup water

TOPPING INGREDIENTS

1	ripe banana, chopped
2	tbsp shredded coconut
1/4	cup Blueberries
1/4	cup Strawberries
1/4	cup Blackberries
1/4	cup Chopped dates
1/4	cup Buckwheat groats
1/4	cup Chopped kiwi
1/4	cup Chopped mango

INSTRUCTIONS

First blend the frozen bananas with the vanilla extract, cinnamon and water until you get banana milk.

You may need to let the bananas thaw for 15-30 minutes before blending.

Next add the topping ingredients into a huge bowl and mix well, pour the banana milk over top and sprinkle with shredded coconut.

All the topping ingredients are optional. If you dont like some of them, use something else or omit it.

BANANA CREPES

SERVINGS	PREP TIME	TOTAL TIME
1	15 MINUTES	12 HOURS

CREPE INGREDIENTS

8   ripe bananas

1/4   cup water

SAUCE INGREDIENTS

8   Medjool dates, pitted

2   tbsp cacao or carob powder

1/4   cup water

TOPPING INGREDIENTS

Chopped banana

Berries

Chopped dates

Cacao nibs

Buckwheat groats

Coconut flakes

INSTRUCTIONS

Blend the bananas and water and pour into 4 small circles, about 4-6 inches diameter onto parchment paper and place in dehydrator at 115°F for 12 hours. Once dehydrated, peel off of the sheets and set aside. If you don't have a dehydrator, read the section "Dehydrating Without A Dehydrator".

For the chocolate sauce, soak the medjool dates in water until soft for an hour or so. Then combine the ingredients in a high speed blender and blend on high until smooth.

To assemble, take your crepes and fill them with whatever you desire or have on hand, roll them like a burrito and add more of the filling to the top. Drizzle with chocolate sauce and serve.

COCONUT YOGURT

SERVINGS	PREP TIME	TOTAL TIME
1	10 MINUTES	2 HOURS

YOGURT INGREDIENTS

- 1 cup coconut milk
- 1 tbsp lemon juice
- 1/2 tsp probiotic powder (optional)
- 1/4 tsp pink salt or fine grain sea salt
- 1 tbsp agave nectar or other sweeteners

TOPPING INGREDIENTS

Mixed berries

Coconut flakes

Buckwheat froats

Mulberries

Oats

INSTRUCTIONS

Add all ingredients into a high speed blender and blend on low, increase the speed gradually until the yogurt is very smooth.

Spoon the yogurt into an air-tight container and chill in the fridge for at least a couple of hours.

Top with berries, coconut flakes, buckwheat groats, mulberries, oats or whatever your heart desires :P

This is also amazing in parfaits, banana ice-cream or a topping for raw soups or mexican dishes, like sour cream.

Store bought coconut yogurt is great as well if you don't have the time or access to young thai coconuts.

CHOCOLATE PUDDING

SERVINGS
1

PREP TIME
5 MINUTES

COOK TIME
0 MINUTES

BASE INGREDIENTS

5   bananas, chopped
2   tbsp cacao or carob powder
1/4   cup water

TOPPING INGREDIENTS

1   banana, sliced
1   tbsp Raw Granola
      (in snacks section)
1   tbsp shredded coconut

INSTRUCTIONS

First take your 5 bananas, water and cacao or carob powder and place in blender.

Process on low until consistency is smooth and place in a serving bowl.

Top with your sliced banana, raw granola and shredded coconut. You can use whatever toppings you like.

You can also substitute frozen bananas and make chocolate banana nice cream the same way!

RAW ØATMEAL

SERVINGS	PREP TIME	COOK TIME
1	5 MINUTES	0 MINUTES

BASE INGREDIENTS

2	apples, cored & chopped
4	Medjool dates, pitted & chopped
4	bananas

TOPPING INGREDIENTS

Cinnamon

Apple chunks

Banana slices

Chopped dates

Buckwheat groats

INSTRUCTIONS

First take your base ingredients: apples, bananas and dates. Place in blender or food processor.

Process on low until it is a oatmeal like consistency, about 30 seconds.

Place your oatmeal in a bowl and top with more dates, banana slices and apple chunks.

You can also add buckwheat groats, coconut or whatever else you like.

Sprinkle with cinnamon and enjoy.

ACAI BOWL

SERVINGS	PREP TIME	COOK TIME
1	5 MINUTES	0 MINUTES

INGREDIENTS

3-5	frozen bananas
1/2	frozen mango
1	cup coconut water
1/2	cup frozen berries
1	fresh ripe banana
1	Medjool date
2	tbsp acai powder
1	tbsp coconut flakes
1	kiwi
1/2	ripe mango
~	Sprinkle of cinnamon

INSTRUCTIONS

Blend frozen bananas, mangoes, acai powder and coconut water until there are no visible chunks and pour into jar.

Chop up the ripe banana, medjool date, kiwi and mango.

Add chopped fruit, frozen berries as well as your coconut flakes and use it to garnish the top of your acai bowl.

Sprinkle with cinnamon and ENJOY!

Acai bowls are great to make when you have lots of bits and pieces of leftover fruit that you don't really know what to do with.

I swear the best acai bowls I have ever made have consisted of the most random ingredients - so no worries if you don't have all of these on hand.

Just use what you have!

FIG & DATE OVERNIGHT OATMEAL

SERVINGS	PREP TIME	TOTAL TIME
1	10 MINUTES	30 MINUTES

INGREDIENTS

1   cup steel cut oats
1   cup dates, chopped
1   cup dried figs, chopped
4   cups water

INSTRUCTIONS

Prepare the dates and figs by chopping them.

In a slow cooker, combine all ingredients and set to low heat. Cover and let cook for 8 to 9 hours.

For the stove top, bring all ingredients to a boil in a medium saucepan, reduce heat to a simmer, cover and cook for 30 minutes.

Stir and remove to serving bowls. This method works best if started before you go to bed. This way your oatmeal will be finished by morning.

Top with extra fresh or dried chopped dates.

PEANUT BUTTER CHOCOLATE OATS

SERVINGS	PREP TIME	TOTAL TIME
1	5 MINUTES	10 MINUTES

INGREDIENTS

2	bananas fresh or frozen
2	cups water
1/2	tbsp peanut butter (regular or powdered)
1	cup rolled oats
~	Pinch of salt (optional)
1	tsp vanilla extract
1	tbsp cacao or carob powder

TOPPING OPTIONS

Peanut butter, nuts, cacao nibs, coconut flakes, fresh fruit, buckwheat groats, chopped banana

INSTRUCTIONS

In a medium saucepan add in the banana, peanut butter, water and oats stir well to combine.

Bring the mixture to a low boil, reduce heat to a simmer, stirring often for 8-10 minutes.

Remove from heat and stir in the vanilla extract.

Transfer to a bowl and sprinkle with cacao or carob, and salt, which is optional, plus whatever toppings you like.

SWEET POTATO OATS

SERVINGS	PREP TIME	TOTAL TIME
1	10 MINUTES	50 MINUTES

INGREDIENTS

1	cup rolled oats
2	cups water
1	medium sweet potato
2	tbsp maple syrup
1/2	tbsp cinnamon
1	tbsp chopped Medjool dates
1	tbsp shredded coconut

INSTRUCTIONS

First bake your sweet potato by setting your oven to 400°F and baking for 30-45 minutes until soft in the center. Once done, take out of oven and let cool. We usually have a few sweet potatoes already baked and in the fridge for snacks so you can always do this beforehand as well.

Next, start your oats by combining the oats and water in a sauce pan. Bring to a boil and then let simmer for about 5 minutes or until most of the water has evaporated.

While your oats are cooking prepare your potato. Once your sweet potato is cooled you will want to remove the skin, you can either mash your sweet potato or chop it into chunks , I like the chunks.

Once your oats are done, place in a serving bowl and add the sweet potato on top, drizzle with your maple syrup, sprinkle on your cinnamon, you can also add in a few medjool dates or some shredded coconut on top.

CARROT CAKE OATMEAL

SERVINGS	PREP TIME	TOTAL TIME
1	5 MINUTES	15 MINUTES

INGREDIENTS

1	cup rolled oats
2	cups water
3	tbsp maple syrup
3	carrots, shredded
2	tbsp shredded coconut
1/3	cup raisins
1/2	tsp cinnamon
1/4	tsp nutmeg and ground ginger

INSTRUCTIONS

Combine oats and water in a medium sauce pan, bring to a boil. Reduce heat and let simmer 5 minutes until the oats are cooked throughly.

Stir in the remaining ingredients and cook until creamy and all the excess liquid is absorbed, about 5 minutes.

Top with additional raisins, coconut and shredded carrot.

BANANA CHOCOLATE CHIP MUFFINS

MAKES 12 MUFFINS

PREP TIME 10 MINUTES

TOTAL TIME 30 MINUTES

DRY INGREDIENTS

2	cups brown rice flour
1/2	tsp baking soda
1/2	tsp baking powder
1/4	tsp salt

WET INGREDIENTS

1	ripe banana, diced
10	Medjool dates
2	cups water

TOPPINGS

2	tbsp cacao nibs

INSTRUCTIONS

Preheat oven to 375°F. First mix all the dry ingredients in a large bowl until well incorporated. Next take your dates and water and blend until smooth. Mix the date/water mixture with your dry ingredients until there are no chunks and then fold in your diced banana.

Take a non-stick 12 cup muffin tray and equally distribute the batter between the sections. Sprinkle the cacao nibs on top equally on the top and lightly mix into the batter.

Place muffins in oven for 20-30 minutes or until you can stick a toothpick in them that comes out clear.

PUMPKIN MUFFINS

MAKES 12 MUFFINS	PREP TIME 10 MINUTES	TOTAL TIME 30 MINUTES

DRY INGREDIENTS

2	cups whole wheat flour
1/2	cup brown sugar
1	tsp cinnamon
1	tbsp baking powder
1/2	tsp baking soda

WET INGREDIENTS

15	oz can of pumpkin
1/2	cup water

INSTRUCTIONS

Preheat oven to 375°F. Whisk the flour, brown sugar, cinnamon, baking powder, baking soda and salt in a large mixing bowl.

Mix in the can of pumpkin and water. Spoon the batter evenly in to a non-stick 12 cup muffin tray.

Bake for 25-30 minutes or until you can stick a toothpick in them that comes out clear.

FLUFFY LEMON PANCAKES

MAKES 4-6 PANCAKES	PREP TIME 10 MINUTES	TOTAL TIME 15 MINUTES

INGREDIENTS

1 1/2   cups flour
2   tsp baking powder
3   ripe bananas
3   Medjool dates
1   cup water
1/2   cup club soda
1/2   tsp vanilla
~   pinch of salt
~   zest of 1 lemon

TOPPINGS

Sliced banana
Blueberries
Cinnamon
Maple syrup

INSTRUCTIONS

Mix together the flour, baking powder and salt in a medium bowl.

Add the water, club soda, dates, vanilla and bananas into a blender and blend on high until smooth.

Stir the banana mixture into the dry ingredients just until combined. Add lemon zest and lightly stir into batter.

Heat a non-stick griddle over medium heat. When it is hot, ladle pancake mixture onto the griddle, using 1/4 cup per pancake, allowing space for them to spread.

When bubbles form on the surface, use a spatula to flip them over. Cook until lightly browned.

Repeat with the remaining batter. Add toppings and serve.

BLUEBERRY BRAN MUFFINS

MAKES 12
MUFFINS

PREP TIME
10 MINUTES

TOTAL TIME
30 MINUTES

INGREDIENTS

1 1/3	cups flour
1	cup wheat bran
1/2	cup sugar
1 1/4	cup non-dairy milk
1/2	cup apple sauce
1	tsp baking soda
2	tbsp ground flax seed
1/2	tsp cinnamon
1/8	tsp salt
1/2	cup blueberries

INSTRUCTIONS

Preheat oven to 350°F. In a large mixing bowl mix the flour, bran, sugar, baking soda, cinnamon and salt. Once the dry ingredients are combined well add in the non-dairy milk, apple sauce and flax seed. Slowly fold in the blueberries as a final step.

Pour the mixture in to a non-stick 12 cup muffin tray and bake for 20-30 minutes or until you can pierce it with a toothpick and it comes out clear.

For a decorative effect, just place the blueberries on the top after you have poured the batter in to the muffin tins instead of folding them in to the batter.

HASHBROWNS

| MAKES 6-8 HASHBROWNS | PREP TIME 15 MINUTES | TOTAL TIME 30 MINUTES |

INGREDIENTS

3-4	lbs potatoes, chopped in chunks
1	tsp salt
1/2	tsp pepper
1	tsp onion powder
1	tsp garlic powder
2	tbsp water

INSTRUCTIONS

Add potatoes and half of the salt into a large pot, cover with water and bring to a boil. Once the water is boiling reduce heat to a simmer, cover and cook for 10-15 minutes or until potatoes are parboiled. Make sure they do not become tender and fall apart, watch them closely. We still want them cooked but firm.

Drain the potatoes and preheat your oven to 400°F. Add the potatoes, remaining salt, spices, pepper and water to a food processor and pulse until chopped into small pieces.

Take a golf ball size of the potato mash and roll it into a ball with your hands and place on a baking tray lined with parchment paper. Do this over and over again until you have all the potato mixture gone. Press the potato balls down with a spatula so they are flat like a patty.

Bake for 20 minutes in the oven, take them out and flip them over using a spatula, bake for another 10 minutes until brown. Allow to cool before serving.

MANGO STICKY RICE

SERVINGS	PREP TIME	TOTAL TIME
1	5 MINUTES	30 MINUTES

INGREDIENTS

1   cup of coconut milk
1   ripe mango
2   Medjool dates, chopped
1/2   cup uncooked brown rice
~   Sesame seeds
~   Pinch of salt (optional)

INSTRUCTIONS

First rinse and drain your brown rice. Combine your coconut milk, dates and rice in a pot, bring to a slow boil, reduce to a simmer for half hour or until all of the milk is absorbed.

Once your rice is done add into a bowl.

Score your mango into squares and scoop on top of the rice/milk mixture.

Garnish with sesame seeds and flavor with a pinch of sea salt, if you wish.

LIGHT
LUNCHES

→

FIESTA SALAD

SERVINGS	PREP TIME	COOK TIME
4-6	30 MINUTES	0 MINUTES

SALAD INGREDIENTS

15	oz can black beans, rinsed and drained
15	oz can kidney beans, rinsed and drained
15	oz can cannellini beans, rinsed and drained
1	yellow bell pepper, chopped
1	red bell pepper, chopped
10	oz package frozen corn kernels
1	red onion, chopped
1/4	cup fresh cilantro, chopped

DRESSING INGREDIENTS

1/2	cup red wine vinegar
1	lime, juice of
2	tbsp maple syrup
1	tbsp salt
1	clove garlic, minced
1	tbsp ground cumin
1/2	tbsp crushed red pepper
1/2	tsp chili powder

INSTRUCTIONS

Take the salad ingredients and combine in a large bowl.

Mix the dressing ingredients in a separate small bowl until well combined.

Pour dressing over salad and let sit and marinate for at least 1 hour before serving.

This salad is great by itself but also try it over rice, on a burrito bowl, in tacos, with baked corn tortilla chips or well, basically anything :).

CREAMY POTATO SALAD

SERVINGS	PREP TIME	TOTAL TIME
2	5 MINUTES	20 MINUTES

INGREDIENTS

2	lbs russet potatoes, peeled & diced
2	tbsp red onion, diced
2	stalks celery, diced
1	large ripe avocado
2	tbsp brown mustard
1	tsp dried dill
1	tsp apple cider vinegar
1/4	tsp salt
1/2	tsp maple syrup
1/4	cup water
~	black pepper, to taste

INSTRUCTIONS

Add the potatoes to a large stock pot and bring to a boil, cook until tender when pricked with a fork, drain and set aside.

Combine the avocado, mustard, dill, apple cider vinegar, water, maple syrup and salt and mash together in a large bowl until well incorporated.

Mix together potatoes with dressing, add in diced onion and celery and top with black pepper.

Let chill in the fridge for 30 minutes to 1 hr.

SIMPLE SUSHI BOWL

SERVINGS	PREP TIME	TOTAL TIME
1	10 MINUTES	30 MINUTES

INGREDIENTS

1   cup uncooked short grain rice

1/2 cucumber, peeled & diced

1   carrot, shredded

1/2 avocado, cubed

~   sesame seeds, to taste

~   tamari, wasabi & pickled ginger (optional), to taste

INSTRUCTIONS

Rinse and drain your brown rice and combine with 2 Cups of water in a small sauce pan, bring to a boil, reduce heat to low and cook until all the water is absorbed, about 30 minutes.

While the rice is cooking peel, dice and prepare your vegetables.

Once the rice is done and has cooled for a bit transfer to a serving bowl.

Add the vegetables, sesame seeds and whatever else you like on top.

Serve with wasabi, tamari and pickled ginger if you like!

PESTO VEGGIE SANDWICH

SERVINGS
1

PREP TIME
10 MINUTES

COOK TIME
0 MINUTES

INGREDIENTS

- 2   pieces high quality bread* or wrap
- ~   Cucumber slices, sun-dried tomato, tomato slices, roasted red pepper, spinach or greens, red onion, roasted eggplant, artichoke hearts, zucchini, olives, sprouts

HUMMUS INGREDIENTS

- 1   can chickpeas, rinsed & drained
- 1/2   cup fresh basil
- 1   large garlic clove, minced
- ~   water (as needed)
- 1   tsp balsamic vinegar
- 1   tsp tamari
- 1/2   a lemon, juice
- ~   salt & ground black pepper, to taste

INSTRUCTIONS

For the hummus, combine all the ingredients in your blender and blend on low until smooth. You will want to slowly add in the water at the end, until everything is blended together.

Take a few tbsp of the hummus and spread over both sides of the bread. Add whatever veggies you like to the sandwich and cut in half to serve.

Keep the leftover hummus in the fridge in a sealed container for up to one week or you can freeze it.

In the picture we used cucumber, tomato, avocado, mixed greens and red onion.

*We like to use a sprouted grain bread like Ezekiel Low Sodium.

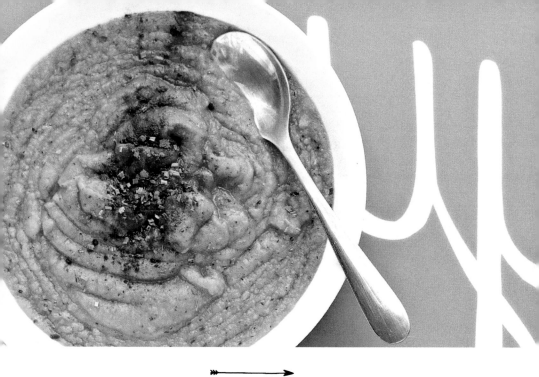

SWEET POTATO SOUP

SERVINGS	PREP TIME	TOTAL TIME
4-6	10 MINUTES	30 MINUTES

INGREDIENTS

1	small onion, cut into chunks
2	garlic cloves, minced
1	tsp thyme
1	tsp cumin
3	lbs sweet potato, peeled & chopped
2	cups vegetable stock
2	cups coconut milk
~	sprinkle of cinnamon

INSTRUCTIONS

Preheat oven to 450°F. Toss the sweet potato, garlic and onion in salt and seasonings and spread out on a large baking sheet lined with parchment paper.

Roast for 25 minutes or until lightly browned and cooked through. Once the potatoes are done add them to your blender along with the vegetable stock and coconut milk. Blend on high until smooth and creamy.

Add additional salt, black pepper and cinnamon before serving if you wish.

MIXED MEXICAN SALAD

SERVINGS	PREP TIME	COOK TIME
1	10 MINUTES	0 MINUTES

SALAD INGREDIENTS

- 1   head romaine lettuce, chopped
- 1/2   cup corn
- 1   medium tomato, chopped
- 1/8   red onion, diced
- 1/2 r   ed pepper, sliced
- ~   small handful of cilantro, chopped
- 1/2   avocado, cubed

DRESSING INGREDIENTS

- 1/2   avocado
- 1   small zucchini
- 1/2   jalapeno pepper, deseeded
- 1   lime, juice of

INSTRUCTIONS

First chop up your lettuce and combine with the rest of the salad ingredients in a large bowl.

Place all your dressing ingredients in your blender and blend on medium-high until creamy and smooth.

Drizzle your dressing over the salad and enjoy.

SIMPLE TACO SALAD

SERVINGS	PREP TIME	TOTAL TIME
1	10 MINUTES	0 MINUTES

INGREDIENTS

4-5	cups spring greens, chopped
1	avocado
3	Roma tomatoes, diced
1/2	bunch cilantro, minced
1/2	red pepper, diced
1	mango, diced
1	cup beans, cooked (pinto or black)
1	cup corn
1	green onion, chopped
1	lime, juice of
1/2	tsp garlic powderr
1/2	tsp cumin
1/2	tsp salt (optional)

INSTRUCTIONS

Place your greens, tomato, cilantro, bell pepper and scallions in a large mixing bowl and toss with the juice of half the lime.

Take your beans, corn, mango, garlic powder, cumin, salt and the remaining lime juice and mix together until it is well incorporated and spoon over the top of the salad.

Top the salad with avocado and serve right away.

Sometimes I add hot sauce or pico de gallo to the top as well. Enjoy!

EPIC RAW SALAD

SERVINGS	PREP TIME	TOTAL TIME
2	10 MINUTES	0 MINUTES

SALAD INGREDIENTS

4	cups spring greens, chopped
1	head romaine, chopped
2	Roma tomatoes, diced
1/2	cucumber, diced
1	zucchini, shredded
1	carrot, shredded
2	tbsp purple sauerkraut
1/2	small avocado, cubed
2	scallions (green onion), diced

DRESSING INGREDIENTS

1/4	cup tahini
1/4	cup water
1	tsp maple syrup
1/2	tbsp apple cider vinegar
1	garlic clove
1	tsp cumin
1/2	lemon, juice of
1/4	tsp salt

INSTRUCTIONS

Prepare all the salad ingredients as directed and arrange in a bowl. Take the dressing ingredients and blend thoroughly in a blender until well incorporated. Pour the dressing over the salad and enjoy.

Any leftover dressing keeps well in the fridge for up to a week. I normally will double the recipe and use this throughout the week on dressings and as a veggie or potato wedge dip.

MEDITERRANEAN SALAD

SERVINGS	PREP TIME	TOTAL TIME
1	10 MINUTES	0 MINUTES

SALAD INGREDIENTS

2	cups spring greens
1	medium tomato, diced
1/2	cucumber, diced
5	olives, diced

DRESSING INGREDIENTS

1/2	cup dried cherries
4	Medjool dates
2	tbsp balsamic vinegar
1/2	cup water

HUMMUS INGREDIENTS

4	small zucchinis
1/4	cup tahini
1	lemon, juice of
2	garlic cloves
1/4	tsp sea salt
2	tsp cumin

INSTRUCTIONS

Chop up all salad ingredients and set aside in a huge mixing bowl. Place cherries and medjool dates in a glass container and pour the 1/2 Cup water over them (make sure you cover all the fruit, we will be using this water in the dressing).

Let soak 3-5 hours or until soft. Place soaked cherries and dates in blender along with the reserved water, balsamic vinegar and blend on high until well incorporated. Set aside.

Take all of the ingredients for the hummus and blend until there are no visible chunks.

Toss the salad with the cherry vinaigrette and top with a dollop of the hummus.

THAI CRUNCH SALAD

SERVINGS	PREP TIME	TOTAL TIME
2	10 MINUTES	0 MINUTES

SALAD INGREDIENTS

4	cups Napa cabbage, shredded
2	cups red cabbage, shredded
1/2	cucumber, deseeded & julienned
1/2	cup carrots, shredded
1/2	cup shelled edamame
3	green onions, diced
1/4 c up	cilantro, minced

DRESSING INGREDIENTS

- 1/4 cup creamy peanut butter
- 2 tbsp rice vinegar
- 1 tbsp lime juice
- 1 tbsp tamari
- 2 tbsp maple syrup
- 2 garlic cloves
- 1 tsp ginger, minced
- 1 tsp salt
- 1/4 tsp red pepper flakes

INSTRUCTIONS

Prepare salad ingredients and toss together in a large bowl. Take all the dressing ingredients and blend on high in blender until well incorporated. Toss the dressing with the salad and enjoy.

CREAMY BALSAMIC SALAD

SERVINGS	PREP TIME	COOK TIME
2	10 MINUTES	0 MINUTES

INGREDIENTS

4   cups spring greens
2   tbsp tahini
2   tbsp balsamic vinegar
1   tbsp maple syrup
1   tbsp brown mustard
~   cracked black pepper

SALAD TOPPINGS

1/4   cup corn
1/2   avocado
1/2   zucchini chopped

INSTRUCTIONS

Chop greens and place in a large bowl.

Whisk together the tahini, balsamic vinegar, maple syrup and brown mustarduntil smooth and toss with greens. Add salad toppings.

Season with fresh cracked black pepper if you wish.

RAW GAZPACHO

SERVINGS	PREP TIME	TOTAL TIME
1	15 MINUTES	0 MINUTES

BASE INGREDIENTS

4	ataulfo mangoes
2	cups orange juice
1/2	medium avocado

TOPPING INGREDIENTS

1/2	tomato, diced
1	tbsp diced red onion
1/2	mango, diced
1/2	medium avocado
~	chopped cilantro

INSTRUCTIONS

Scoop the flesh of the mangoes out, reserving one half for topping and place in a blender with the avocado and orange juice.

Blend until smooth. Dice the other half of the mango and use to top the soup.

Add other toppings such as tomato, red onion, the rest of the avocado and cilantro.

Serve right away.

PINEAPPLE UN-FRIED RICE

SERVINGS	PREP TIME	COOK TIME
2	15 MINUTES	0 MINUTES

SAUCE INGREDIENTS

1	lime, uice of
2	tbsp nama shoyu or coconut aminos
2	tbsp water
2	garlic cloves, minced
~	pinch of red pepper flakes
1/2	tsp ginger

BASE INGREDIENTS

2	cups cauliflower, processed
2	cups pineapple, chopped
2	scallions, chopped
1/2	cup mushrooms, chopped
1	handful of cilantro, minced
1/2	red pepper, chopped
1	small zucchini, chopped
1	carrot, chopped

INSTRUCTIONS

In a food processor with the S blade, process the cauliflower until it becomes a rice like consistency. We used purple caulflower for the picture. How cool!

Chop the rest of the base ingredients in to a bowl with the cauliflower rice.

In a small mixing bowl, combine the sauce ingredients and stir well. Pour the sauce over the rice and mix together well.

Top with cilantro and sesame seeds and enjoy.

PASTA
NIGHT

➤

THAI PEANUT NOODLES

SERVINGS	PREP TIME	TOTAL TIME
2	10 MINUTES	10 MINUTES

SAUCE INGREDIENTS

4	tbsp powdered peanut butter
1	tbsp tamari
3	tbsp water
1/4	tsp garlic powder
1/4	tsp red pepper
1/4	tsp ginger powder
1	tbsp maple syrup

BASE INGREDIENTS

8	oz rice noodles

TOPPINGS

1/4	cup carrots, shredded
1/2	red bell pepper, julienned
1	cup baby broccoli
1/2	cup cilantro, minced
1/4	cup bean sprouts
2	scallions, diced
1	lime wedge

INSTRUCTIONS

Bring a pot filled with water to a boil and drop rice noodles in, cook according to directions, usually 10 minutes and run under cold water to cool. Drain and set aside.

Take your broccoli, red bell pepper and carrots and sauté in a bit of water until tender.

Place all the sauce ingredients in a bowl and whisk together.

Combine your noodles and sauce in a bowl and add in your sautéed vegetables, cilantro, and scallions.

Top with bean sprouts and fresh squeezed lime juice.

MEAT-LESS BALLS

SERVINGS	PREP TIME	TOTAL TIME
4	20 MINUTES	45 MINUTES

INGREDIENTS

2   cups red lentils, rinsed & drained

4   cups water

1/2   onion, minced

3   garlic cloves, minced

1   carrot, shredded

1   stalk celery, minced

2   cups bread crumbs or Toast 6 slices Ezekiel 4:9 bread)

2   tbsp ground flax seeds + 2 tbsp warm water

2   tbsp tamari or soy sauce

1   tsp each garlic powder, oregano, basil, paprika, chili powder

INSTRUCTIONS

First combine the ground flax with the 2 tbsp warm water so that it can sit and turn into jelly. Next take your lentils and water in a large pot, bring to a boil, reduce heat to simmer and let cool until the water is absorbed, about 20 minutes.

While the lentils are cooking take your onion, garlic, celery and carrot and simmer in about 1/4 cup of water until slightly cooked. Next add in the soy sauce and seasonings with salt and stir to combine.

When your lentils are finished cooking place them in a food processor, add in the onion, garlic, celery and carrot mix and process until combined. Next add in your flax seed mix and slowly add in the bread crumbs 1/4 cup at a time, processing in between.

Once all is combined place in a large mixing bowl and let sit in the fridge for an hour or until cooled to the touch. Once cooled take a scoop at a time and roll into balls of whatever size you like.

SPAGHETTI

PREP TIME
10 MINUTES

TOTAL TIME
30 MINUTES

MARINARA INGREDIENTS

You may use store bought marinara, which is what I usually do, or here is a simple recipe I use when I have the ingredients on hand.

15	oz can diced tomatoes
15	oz can tomato sauce
6	oz can tomato paste
2	tbsp maple syrup
1/2	tsp basil
1/2	tsp oregano
1/2	tsp black pepper
1/2	tsp salt
1	tsp crushed red pepper flakes

BASE INGREDIENTS

12	oz spaghetti noodles, cooked

INSTRUCTIONS

Throw and mix all ingredients into a sauce pan, bring to a boil, turn heat to low and simmer for 20-30 minutes.

Serve over cooked spaghetti noodles and top with the meat-less balls on the previous page.

CREAMY ALFREDO PASTA

SERVINGS	PREP TIME	COOK TIME
1	20 MINUTES	0 MINUTES

BASE INGREDIENTS

1   large zucchini, spiralized

SAUCE INGREDIENTS

2   cups cauliflower, chopped
2   garlic cloves
2   tbsp hemp seeds
2   tbsp nutritional yeast (optional)
1/2 lemon, juice of
1/4 tsp salt
1/4 cup water

INSTRUCTIONS

First spiralize your zucchini and place the noodles in a bowl.

For the sauce we will be adding everything into a blender.

Blend on high until the sauce comes out smooth and creamy. Take your sauce and mix it with the noodles until they are evenly coated.

You can top this with fresh basil, tomatoes or other vegetables you like.

RED PEPPER SPAGHETTI

SERVINGS	PREP TIME	TOTAL TIME
1	20 MINUTES	0 MINUTES

PASTA INGREDIENTS

3-5   zucchini, spiralized
1-2   carrots, spiralized

SAUCE INGREDIENTS

1/2   cup sun-dried tomatoes, soaked
2   Medjool dates, soaked
2-3   Roma tomatoes
1   garlic clove
3-5   leaves fresh basil
1/2   red pepper, deseeded
~   pinch of salt (optional)
1/4   cup nutritonal yeast (optional)

INSTRUCTIONS

One of the great things about raw food is that the recipes can be very easy to make. Like this one!

Soak the sun-dried tomatoes and the pitted dates for at least 1 hour or until soft. Place all the sauce ingredients in a blender and blend on high until smooth.

Pour over zucchini noodles sprialized and top with extra basil. Before you spiralize the zucchinis, you can use a vegetable peeler and take off the skin for a more authentic pasta look.

There are so many options for spiralizing veggies. We like the spiralizer style that feeds the vegetables horizontally and uses a hand crank. They are typically white in color

QUICK
BITES

→

MANGO TACOS

SERVINGS
3-4

PREP TIME
20 MINUTES

COOK TIME
0 MINUTES

TACO INGREDIENTS

5-6	mangoes, diced
2	large tomatoes, diced
1	cup corn
1	red pepper, diced
1/2	cup jicama, diced
1	small red onion, minced
~	Cilantro, minced
~	jalapeno, deseeded & minced
1	head romaine

DRESSING INGREDIENTS

1	tsp each chili powder, cumin
1	lime, juice of
1	garlic cloved, crushed
1	tbsp agave nectar
1/4	cup red wine vinegar (or water)

SOUR CREAM INGREDIENTS

1	cup hemp seeds
1/2	cup water (approximately)
1/2	lemon, juice of
1	tsp apple cider vinegar

INSTRUCTIONS

First, we will assemble our taco filling. Take your mangoes, tomatoes, corn, bell pepper, jicama, onion, cilantro and jalapeño and toss together in a large mixing bowl.

Next take your dressing ingredients and whisk together in a bowl. Then take your dressing and mix with the taco filling until well incorporated and set aside.

For the sour cream, blend all ingredients on high in a blender until smooth. It's best if you let this refrigerate a few hours before using.

To assemble the tacos, fill a romaine leaf with the filling, top with avocado and drizzle with sour cream.

HONEYLESS BBQ WINGS

SERVINGS	PREP TIME	DEHYDRATING
4	20 MINUTES	TIME 8 HOURS

INGREDIENTS

1	head cauliflower, broke into pieces

HEMP RANCH INGREDIENTS

1/2	cup hemp seeds
1/2	cup water
1	tbsp apple cider vinegar
1/2	lemon, juice of
1/4	tsp salt
1	tsp agave nectar
1	garlic clove
1	tsp dill

BBQ SAUCE INGREDIENTS

10	Medjool dates, pitted (soaked 2 hours)
1/4	cup sun-dried tomatoes (soaked 2 hours)
1	tbsp chili powder
1	tsp cayenne
1/2	cup water
2	garlic cloves
1	tbsp apple cider binegar
2	tbsp hemp seeds or tahini

INSTRUCTIONS

Allow the dates and sun-dried tomatoes about 2 hours to soak in water until they are soft.

Take the BBQ sauce ingredients and blend until smooth. Dip the cauliflower pieces into the BBQ sauce and spread evenly over each piece with your hands.

To make the hemp ranch dressing, just blend all of the ingredients together.

Align the bites on your dehydrator tray and dehydrate on 115°F for 8 hours. If you don't have a dehydrator, read the section "Dehydrating Without A Dehydrator".

RAW FALAFEL & TZATZIKI DIP

SERVINGS
8-12 PIECES

PREP TIME
30 MINUTES

DEHYDRATING
TIME: 8 HOURS

FALAFEL INGREDIENTS

2	cups carrots
2	cups cauliflower
1/4	cup dates, pitted & soaked
1/2	cup sun-dried tomatoes, soaked
1/2	onion, chopped
1/4	cup parsley, chopped
1	tsp dried celery salt
1	tbsp cumin (optional)
1	tbsp curry powder (optional)
1	tsp pepper (optional)

TZATZIKI INGREDIENTS

1	young Thai coconut (meat & water)
1	lemon, juice of
1/2	cup cucumber, diced
1/4	cup dill, diced
1	garlic clove (optional)

INSTRUCTIONS

In a food processor shred the carrots, remove them and then process the cauliflower lightly so that it is not completely broken down, some florets still visible. Remove the cauliflower and set aside along with the carrots.

Process the sun-dried tomatoes with the S-blade before adding the pitted dates along with any spices. Continue processing until a dough-like ball forms. Now, add carrots and cauliflower. Process further until it is nearly finished mixing and everything is the same consistency.

Add in onion and parsley. Pulse and mix the contents. Remove the mixture from food processor and form in to balls or flatten them slightly. Dehydrate for 8 hours.

For the dip, blend the ingredients, except for the dill and cucumber, and slowly add coconut water to achieve the desired consistency. Stir dill and cucumber in and serve. Dip the falafels and enjoy, or put them on a lettuce leaf or cabbage leaf and fill that with more lettuce, tomato and drizzle the dip on top.

CHINESE LETTUCE WRAPS

| MAKES 8-12 WRAPS | PREP TIME 30 MINUTES | DEHYDRATING TIME 12 HOURS |

BASE INGREDIENTS

1/2	head cauliflower (2 cups)
2	medium carrots, shredded
1/2	red onion, chopped
3	stalks celery, chopped
8	Medjool dates, pitted & soaked
1	tsp Chinese 5 spice
~	salt & red pepper flakes (optional)

SAUCE INGREDIENTS

2	mangoes
4	dates

TOPPING INGREDIENTS

Bean sprouts
Chopped mushrooms
Scallions
Diced red/yellow peppers
Shredded carrots
Iceberg lettuce (for wraps)

INSTRUCTIONS

In your food processor, process the celery, onion and cauliflower into small pieces and place in a large mixing bowl. Add the carrots, Chinese five spice, salt and pepper if you wish and toss until all evenly coated.

Next add your dates to your food processor and mix until they are a paste. Add them to the mixing bowl of veggies and mix well until incorporated. Next we are going to put all of this back into the food processor to mix it all very well and get it into a thick and chunky mixture that sticks together.

Spread the entire mixture out on a piece of parchment paper placed on your dehydrator tray. Dehydrate this at 115°F for 12 hours. When your mix is dehydrated and can kind of crumble apart like granola would, that is the consistency we want. It doesn't have to be completely dried.

For the sauce place everything in your blender and blend until smooth. Place your base mixture into a lettuce cup, add whatever toppings you like and top with sauce.

CHEESY KALE CHIPS

SERVINGS	PREP TIME	DEHYDRATING
4	20 MINUTES	TIME 12 HOURS

BASE INGREDIENTS

1	large bunch of kale

CHEESE INGREDIENTS

1	cup cashews (soaked 2 hours) or 1 cup hemp seeds
1	red pepper, deseeded and chopped
1/2	lemon, juice of
2	tbsp nutritional yeast
1	tsp chili powder
1/2	tsp cayenne
1/2	tsp Himalayan sea salt

INSTRUCTIONS

Rinse the kale and pat dry. Remove the stems and tear into bite size pieces. Make sure the kale is pretty dry before coating.

Next blend together your soaked cashews or hemp seeds, bell pepper, lemon juice, nutritional yeast, and seasonings on high until smooth.

Transfer kale to a large bowl and mix well with your cheese sauce. It's best to use your hands to ensure the leaves are well coated.

Place the kale on the dehydrator trays. Dehydrate at 115°F overnight or until coating is dry. This usually takes around 12 hours. If you don't have a dehydrator, read the section "Dehydrating Without A Dehydrator".

Once done, you can place them in an air tight container or eat them all immediately, which is what usually happens.

COMFORT
FOODS

→

CORNBREAD

SERVINGS	PREP TIME	COOK TIME
6	10 MINUTES	20 MINUTES

INGREDIENTS

1	cup cornmeal
1	cup pastry flour
1	tbsp baking powder
1	cup organic soymilk
1/4	cup unsweetened applesauce
1/4	cup pure maple syrup

INSTRUCTIONS

Preheat oven to 400°F. In a large mixing bowl whisk the cornmeal, flour and baking powder.

Add the soy milk, applesauce and maple syrup on top. Use a spatula and stir until just combined.

Pour the batter into a non-stick loaf pan.

Bake for approximately 20 minutes or until a toothpick inserted into the center comes out clean.

Enjoy this delicious cornbread with the potato curry chili recipe!

RED PEPPER MAC N CHEESE

SERVINGS	PREP TIME	COOK TIME
2	10 MINUTES	30 MINUTES

SAUCE INGREDIENTS

1	red pepper, roasted
1	clove garlic
1/2	lemon, juice of
2	tbsp hemp seeds
4	tbsp nutritional yeast
1/4	tsp cayenne
1/2	tsp salt
1/4	cup water

BASE INGREDIENTS

12	oz elbow style noodles (brown rice, quinoa or corn)

TOPPINGS

Handful chopped basil

INSTRUCTIONS

Preheat oven to broil, cut the red pepper in half and place with the inside down on highest rack with a pan underneath to catch drippings.

Watching closely you just want to char the outside of the pepper until it's slightly black.

Once the pepper is roasted, take out of oven and run under cool water as you peel off the skin and discard the seeds and stem.

Place the pepper along with all the other sauce ingredients in blender and blend until smooth and creamy.

Cook your noodles according to package. Once cooked combine with the sauce in a pan and simmer until the sauce thickens. Top with basil and enjoy!

BURRITO

| SERVINGS 2-3 | PREP TIME 10 MINUTES | COOK TIME 45 MINUTES |

FILLING INGREDIENTS

Corn
Diced tomato
Salsa
Lime juice
Diced avocado
Diced red onion

BEAN MIX INGREDIENTS

1 15 oz can romano or pinto beans, drained & rinsed
1/3 cup water (from the beans)
1 tbsp rice vinegar
1 tsp chili powder

MAIN INGREDIENTS

10" whole wheat tortillas
1-2 cups uncooked rice

INSTRUCTIONS

Cook the rice in a pot or rice cooker and set aside. Drain the can of beans and catch 1/3 cup of the water. Place the rinsed beans, water, rice vinegar and chili powder in the blender and blend on low till smooth.

Prepare and dice all the filling ingredients. Lay out one tortilla. Use a spatula to spoon out some bean mix on the tortilla in a row. Top with rice and any of the filling ingredients you have on hand or desire.

Once all the ingredients are in the tortilla, roll the burrito by folding the edges over the row of filling. With the sides folded in, use your thumbs to bring up the bottom of the tortilla. Almost like wrapping a present; tuck in the ends while bringing up the bottom flap. Roll the burrito tight while tucking the bottom flap in. You should have a nice burrito pouch now.

Preheat a non-stick pan on low to medium heat with a cover. Place the finished burritos on the pan and cook for 3-4 minutes on both sides until the desired crispiness is achieved.

FRIES

PREP TIME
10 MINUTES

COOK TIME
30 MINUTES

INGREDIENTS

1-2	lbs russet potato
1	tsp garlic powder
1	tsp onion powder
1	tsp chili powder

SAUCE INGREDIENTS

1	red bell pepper
2 s	mall tomatoes
7 or 8	large Medjool dates, pitted
1/2	avocado (optional)

INSTRUCTIONS

Peel and dice the potatoes in to fry shaped wedges. In a large mixing bowl, coat the fries with the garlic, onion and chili powder. Toss until all are coated. Add more powder if you want more flavor.

Preheat oven to 400°F. Place the fries on a pan with parchment paper to avoid using oil or you can place the fries directly on the oven rack and put a pan on a rack below to catch any falling fries. Bake for 30 minutes or until cooked through. Test with a fork to ensure the fries are cooked consistently all the way through. If placing fries directly on the rack, remove using a set of tongs.

While the fries are cooking, place all the sauce ingredients in your blender. Blend until desired consistency is achieved. Add in avocado for a creamier sauce.

If you want crispier fries, put the oven on broil for the last 5 minutes and keep a close eye on them so they do not burn.

BEAN TACOS

SERVINGS	PREP TIME	COOK TIME
1-2	10 MINUTES	15 MINUTES

REFRIED BEANS INGREDIENTS

1	onion, minced
1	jalapeno, deseeded & chopped
1	tbsp garlic, minced
3	cups dry pinto beans, rinsed
1/8	tsp cumin
9	cups water
~	salt (if desired)

TOPPINGS

Shredded lettuce, tomato, salsa, onion, guacamole, olives, peppers

TACOS

Corn tortillas

INSTRUCTIONS

Place all the bean mix ingredients in a slow cooker and mix. Cook on high for 8 hours adding more water if needed.

Once the beans are cooked, strain any excess liquid, mash with a potato masher and they are ready to eat. You can freeze any extras or they are good for up to one week in the fridge.

For the tacos, preheat the oven to 400°F. Spread out an even layer of the beans on to each tortilla and fold in half. These will get crispy and harden when they are in the oven so shape them how you would want a taco to be. Place tacos in the oven for 10-15 minutes. Watch them closely and once they start to harden take them out.

Place desired toppings in the shells and serve with salsa and guacamole.

CHANA MASALA

SERVINGS
2

PREP TIME
10 MINUTES

COOK TIME
30 MINUTES

INGREDIENTS

1   cup uncooked rice

1   yellow onion, diced

3   cups (28 oz canned)
     fire roasted tomatoes

3   cups (2 cans) chickpeas,
     drained & rinsed

1   tsp cumin seeds

1   tbsp fresh ginger, peeled
     & finely chopped

4   garlic cloves, minced

1/2 tsp cayenne pepper

2   tsp garam masala

1   tsp coriander

1   tsp turmeric

1/4 cup water

~   salt to taste (add at the
     end if desired)

INSTRUCTIONS

Cook the rice in either a separate pot or in a rice cooker.

Place a large saucepan over medium heat and lightly toast your cumin seeds for about 1 minute.

Next add in your water, onions, ginger and garlic and sauté until translucent, about 5 minutes. Slowly stir in your spices and let cook for 3 more minutes.

Raise the heat to medium high, add in your tomatoes and chickpeas and bring to a simmer.

Let cook for 15 minutes until all the flavors meld together.

Serve over rice.

MASHED POTATOES & GRAVY

SERVINGS	PREP TIME	COOK TIME
1-2	10 MINUTES	30 MINUTES

INGREDIENTS

5   medium potatoes, peeled & diced

OPTIONAL SIDES

Asparagus

Fire roasted organic corn

Fresh steamed green beans

GRAVY (6 SERVINGS)

6   tbsp organic cornstarch or arrowroot powder

10   vegetable bouillon cubes

1   tsp onion powder

1   tsp garlic powder

1   tsp oregano

1   tsp paprika

INSTRUCTIONS

Mix the dry gravy ingredients together so that it becomes a fine powder. You can do this in a Vitamix, or a coffee grinder. This is a great dry mix to keep on hand and makes it very easy to have an awesome thick vegan gravy in minutes. Store the mixture in a small mason jar or glass container in your spice cupboard. When you are ready to use, just mix 1 tbsp of gravy mix with 1/2 cup of water in a small pan and turn on high. Bring to a boil and continually whisk the mixture until it forms to the thickness you like, around 3 minutes.

For the mashed potatoes, combine your peeled and quartered potatoes with enough water in a large pot to barely cover them. Bring to a boil, lower heat to simmer and cook until they are soft or fall apart with a prick of the fork. Drain and transfer to a large mixing bowl.

Mash your potatoes until smooth. You can add in a little plant milk and that will make them super creamy.

Once your potatoes are done, pour the gravy over top and add some vegetable sides if you like. I love eating this with asparagus, fire roasted organic corn or fresh steamed green beans. Enjoy!

POTATO GNOCCHI

SERVINGS	PREP TIME	COOK TIME
1-2	30 MINUTES	60 MINUTES

INGREDIENTS

4	large russet potatoes
1 - 1½	cups flour
~	Water

INSTRUCTIONS

Preheat oven to 425°F and place potatoes in a single layer on a tray. Cook for 45 minutes. Let sit until cool enough to handle, cut in half and scoop out the flesh. Discard skins. Mash the potatoes with a masher in a large mixing bowl. Bring a large pasta pot filled with water to a slow boil.

Add flour to the mashed potato in 1/4 cup intervals, using your knuckles to press the flour into the potatoes. Once the consistency is firm, start rolling the gnocchi into small balls. We just line them up on a sheet of parchment paper to boil once we're done, you can use a fork to shape the gnocchi.

Use your thumb to roll it down to the end. You will get ridges on one side and a "dimple" on the other side, which holds whatever sauce you cook it in. Repeat until the entire ball of dough has been rolled into gnocchi. When you have all the gnocchi rolled start dropping them one by one into the pot of boiling water. If it rises to the top without falling apart its done. Do this until all the gnocchi is cooked.

You can now serve them in whatever sauce you like. I use the basic marinara sauce in this book or this would also be great in the Mac 'n Cheese sauce or a homemade pesto.

VEGGIE BURGER

MAKES	PREP TIME	COOK TIME
4 BURGERS	10 MINUTES	30 MINUTES

INGREDIENTS

16	oz can chickpeas
1	cup corn
1/2	tsp each: paprika, cumin, garlic powder, cayenne, salt
1/4	cup flour, any kind
4	whole wheat buns

TOPPINGS

Lettuce

Tomato

Onion

Pickles

Ketchup

Red pepper sauce

INSTRUCTIONS

Combine the chickpeas, corn, flour and spices in a food processor and process until well combined. Dust a surface with flour and divide your mixture into 4 equal parts.

Using the flour to keep the mixture from sticking shape and mold them into burger sized patties. Once finished place on a piece of parchment paper and let sit in the fridge for 30 minutes to firm up.

Using a non-stick pan over medium high heat place the patties in the pan and let them brown on each side for about 6-8 minutes. Flip and brown the other side.

Serve on whole wheat buns with tomato, lettuce, onion, pickles or whatever you like.

Enjoy!

RAW MUSHROOM BURGERS

MAKES
4 BURGERS

PREP TIME
10 MINUTES

DEHYDRATING
TIME 24 HOURS

BURGER INGREDIENTS

1	cup mushrooms, chopped
1/2	cup carrots, chopped
1/2	cup zucchini, chopped
3	Medjool dates, chopped
2	sun-dried tomatoes, chopped
1	tbsp nama shoyu or coconut aminos
1	tbsp apple cider vinegar
1	garlic clove
1/2	tbsp chili powder
1/2	tbsp cumin
2	tbsp ground flax

TOPPING INGREDIENTS

Romaine leaves, cut in half

Tomato

Onion

Avocado

Cashew cheese(recipe from the cheesy kale chips)

Sprouts

INSTRUCTIONS

Make sure the dates and sun-dried tomatoes soak for at least 1 hour or until soft.

Combine all of your burger ingredients, minus the flax, in your food processor and process until well combined.

Place the mixture in a large mixing bowl and fold in the ground flax. This mixture will be pretty wet. Form into burger sized patties and place in the dehydrator at 115°F for 12 hours.

If you don't have a dehydrator we have instructions in the information section to use your oven for this recipe.

Check at 12 hours and compact them more into burger form using your hands. Dehydrate another 12 hours checking every 6 hours.

When they are firm and no longer sticky they are ready. Take a burger and place between two sheets of romaine and add in whatever fixings you like and enjoy!

RAW PAD THAI

SERVINGS	PREP TIME	COOK TIME
2	20 MINUTES	0 MINUTES

BASE INGREDIENTS

1/2	red pepper, sliced
1-2	carrots, shredded
1	small handful cilantro, chopped
1/2	cup bean sprouts
3	zucchini, spiralized
1/4	red onion, finely sliced
1/2	lime
~	sesame seeds

SAUCE INGREDIENTS

1/2	red pepper
1	Roma tomato
1/2	cup sun-dried tomatoes, soaked
3	Medjool dates, pitted & soaked
2	tbsp tahini
1	tsp grated fresh ginger
~	pinch of cayenne pepper
1/2	lime, juice of

INSTRUCTIONS

First soak your sun-dried tomatoes and dates for 1 hour or until very soft.

Prep all of your base vegetables and toss in a large bowl. Blend all the sauce ingredients until smooth and pour over the pad thai.

Mix the sauce together with the salad until well coated. Sprinkle with the sesame seeds and squeeze with lime juice.

COUNTRY STYLE
POTATOES

SERVINGS	PREP TIME	COOK TIME
4-6	10 MINUTES	30 MINUTES

INGREDIENTS

1	5lb bag of red potatoes, cut into chunks
4	garlic cloves, minced
1	onion, peeled & chopped
4	bell peppers, deseeded & chopped
1/4	cup vegetable stock
1	tsp cumin
1	tsp chili powder
1	tsp seasoned salt
1/2	tsp cayenne pepper

INSTRUCTIONS

Preheat the oven to 425°F. In a large bowl, toss together the potatoes, garlic, onion, bell peppers, vegetable stock, cayenne pepper, chili powder and cumin.

Sprinkle with a little salt and freshly cracked black pepper.

Pour potatoes into 2 baking sheets lined with parchment paper. Bake for 20 to 25 minutes, shaking the pan twice.

Raise the heat to 500°F and bake until crispy and brown, 15 to 20 minutes, tossing a few times.

If you like to plan in advance, the BEST thing to do with this recipe is prep it the night before and throw all the ingredients in a bag to marinate overnight. You will not regret it!

PEA & POTATO SOUP

SERVINGS
4-6

PREP TIME
10 MINUTES

COOK TIME
30 MINUTES

INGREDIENTS

5	cups vegetable broth or water
1	small onion, diced
3	garlic cloves, minced
1	lb yellow potatoes, peeled & diced
4	stalks celery, diced
1 1/2	cups green split peas, rinsed & drained
1	tbsp each, oregano, basil and thyme
~	salt & black pepper to taste

INSTRUCTIONS

In a large stockpot sauté your onion and garlic in a small amount of broth or water until translucent and fragrant.

Next add in the rest of your ingredients, bring to a boil. reduce heat and simmer for 30 minutes or until the potatoes are soft and the peas have absorbed most of the water.

This soup should be slightly thick.

Add your salt and black pepper just before serving.

To make this super green and vibrant, I blended 2 cups of frozen peas until they were smooth and then stirred that in at the very end.

POTATO CHOWDER

SERVINGS
4-6

PREP TIME
10 MINUTES

COOK TIME
30 MINUTES

INGREDIENTS

1	leek, diced (white part only)
5	garlic cloves, minced
5	thyme sprigs, leaves removed
1/2	small celery root, diced
3	cups cauliflower, chopped
10	small red potatoes
2	tbsp brown mustard
1	tsp seasoning salt or sea salt
~	cracked black pepper
1/2	lime, juice of
1/4	cup nutritional yeast
1	quart vegetable stock

INSTRUCTIONS

In a medium sauce pan saute the leek, garlic and thyme sprigs in a bit of the vegetable stock until fragrant (about 3 minutes).

Add in the rest of the vegetable stock, potatoes, celery root and cauliflower. Bring to a boil, lower heat and cook on low until potatoes are soft (about 10 minutes).

While the soup is cooking, combine the brown mustard, salt, black pepper, lemon juice and nutritional yeast and set aside.

Once the potatoes are soft, ladle half of the soup into your blender and blend on high until smooth. Pour back into pot with the remaining soup, add in your seasoning mix from earlier and cook for an additional 10-15 minutes on low.

Serve with additional thyme sprigs and your favorite salad and enjoy :)

HEARTY CHILI

SERVINGS	PREP TIME	CROCKPOT TIME
4-6	10 MINUTES	8-10 HOURS

INGREDIENTS

1	cup dry kidney beans
1	cup dry kidney beans
1	large onion, chopped
2	garlic cloves, minced
2	tbsp chili powder
1	tbsp ground cumin
1/2	tsp salt
1	tbsp fresh oregano or 1 tsp dried
2	lbs fresh tomatoes, chopped
1 - 2	fresh or dried hot chilies, deseeded and minced
1	cup red lentils
5	stalks of celery, chopped
6	cups water (You may need to add more at the end depending how long you cook it for.)

INSTRUCTIONS

This one is super easy. Once you have rinsed your beans and lentils and picked them over, place all your ingredients in a crock pot on low heat for 8-10 hours.

This is a great meal to prep the night before in the crockpot. Then in the morning you can just turn it on and you don't have to worry about making dinner when you come home!

LOADED BAKED POTATOES

SERVINGS	PREP TIME	COOK TIME
2	10 MINUTES	30 MINUTES

CHEESE SAUCE INGREDIENTS

2	cups cauliflower florets
2	cups water
1	tsp garlic powder
1	tsp onion powder
1/2	tsp dried mustard
1/2	tsp turmeric
1	tsp salt
1/4	cup nutritional yeast
1	tbsp lemon juice

BASE INGREDIENTS

2-3 large russet potatoes

Chili (recipe in book)

Hot sauce (optional)

Chives

INSTRUCTIONS

To make the cheese sauce, combine water and cauliflower in a pot and bring to a boil. Reduce to simmer and remove once cauliflower is tender. Transfer to a blender and add in the remaining ingredients. Blend on high until smooth and transfer to a bowl or storage container

To make the baked potatoes, cover potatoes with aluminum foil and bake for 1 hour or until soft at 450°F.

Take the potatoes out of the foil, cut in half and allow to cool a few minutes.

Add chili, cheese and chives to top.

MADRAS SPICED DHAL

SERVINGS	PREP TIME	COOK TIME
6	10 MINUTES	1 HOUR

MADRAS SPICE INGREDIENTS

1/2	cup coriander seeds
1/3	cup cumin seeds
2	tbsp turmeric
2	tbsp cardamom pods
1	tbsp cayenne pepper
1	tbsp cloves
8	black peppercorns
1	tbsp dried fenugreek leaves

DHAL INGREDIENTS

2	cups red lentils, rinsed
5	medium potatoes, peeled & diced
4	garlic cloves, minced
1	small onion, diced
4	tbsp madras spice mix
1	tsp cinnamon
10	oz package frozen spinach
1	cup carrots, shredded
6	cups water

INSTRUCTIONS

Place all the spice ingredients in a spice grinder or Vitamix and blend until a fine powder forms.

There are also companies that make a madras spice mix, just look in the spices section if you want to make it easy.

The best way to eat lentils is to let them cook for quite a while so this recipe takes a little bit of time the way that I lay it out here but if you are short on time just throw everything in the pot, bring to a boil, reduce heat and simmer for an hour. You can also throw it all in a crockpot before work and when you get home it will be ready.

The long version is so much more worth it though. It produces a very creamy and consistent dahl. First we are going to take our onion and garlic and saute in a bit of water for 5 minutes or until translucent. Then add the rest of the water and lentils, bring to a boil, reduce and let simmer 30 minutes. Next add in your potatoes, carrots, madras spice and let cook another half hour to 45 minutes or until the potatoes are tender and fall apart. Add in your cinnamon and spinach, stir around until spinach is unthawed. Serve over brown rice or by itself. Add salt if desired before serving.

EPIC
DINNERS

➤➤──────────────➤

THAI GREEN CURRY

SERVINGS	PREP TIME	COOK TIME
2	10 MINUTES	30 MINUTES

CURRY INGREDIENTS

2	cups boxed coconut milk*
4	tbsp green curry paste
2	stalks celery, chopped
1	red pepper, chopped
1	zucchini, chopped
5	green onions, chopped
3	cloves garlic, minced
4	cups bok choy, chopped
1	cup water
3-5	kaffir lime leaves or fresh kaffir lime zest (optional)

BASE INGREDIENTS

2	cups uncooked brown rice
4	cups water

INSTRUCTIONS

*I use the boxed coconut milk because it has about 1/4 of the fat compared to the canned, the cooking method we use makes it nice and creamy, the same way it would be if you used the thicker canned milk.

First combine your rice and water in a pan or your rice cooker and cook until done. While the rice is cooking heat the coconut milk, curry paste, kaffir lime leaves and garlic in a pan over medium high heat, bring to a boil and let simmer.

Place the rest of the vegetables and water in another pan over medium heat and sauté until tender, about 5-7 minutes. Watch the coconut milk mixture carefully. We want to boil it down a bit until it is the desired thickness you want.

We usually cook it for 7-10 minutes on a low boil and constantly stir it with a whisk. Once it is thick and fragrant place mix together with your vegetables and let them sit for 5-10 minutes to soak in the flavors. Serve over rice.

POTATO CURRY CHILI

SERVINGS	PREP TIME	CROCKPOT TIME
4-6	10 MINUTES	3-6 HOURS

INGREDIENTS

- 1 lb russet potato, diced
- 1 red pepper, diced
- 1 yellow bell pepper, diced
- 1 large red onion, diced
- 3 garlic cloves, minced
- 1 tbsp curry powder
- 1 tbsp chili powder
- 1 tsp cumin
- 1 tsp cayenne
- 19 oz can black beans, with liquid
- 28 oz can diced tomatoes, with liquid
- 12 oz can niblet corn, with liquid

INSTRUCTIONS

Dice the potato, bell peppers and onions and place in to a slow cooker.

Top with the minced garlic, curry powder and chili powder.

Use a large spoon to stir around so that everything is coated with the powders.

Pour the cans of black beans, diced tomatoes and niblet corn directly in to the slow cooker.

Turn on high for 3-4 hours or on low for 6 hours. Stir periodically and check the potatoes for when they are tender.

ALOO GOBI

SERVINGS	PREP TIME	COOK TIME
4-6	10 MINUTES	40 MINUTES

INGREDIENTS

1	tsp black mustard seeds
1	tsp cumin seeds
3	whole cloves
2	tsp garam masala
1/4	tsp turmeric
3	garlic cloves, minced
1/2	tsp fresh ginger, minced
1	medium onion, minced
4	medium Yukon gold potatoes, peeled & diced
2	cups cauliflower, ciced
2	tbsp water + 1/2 cup water
2	tsp maple syrup
~	salt (optional add before serving)

INSTRUCTIONS

Add the 2 tbsp water, mustard seeds, cumin, cloves, garam masala and turmeric to a pan over medium high heat and sauté the spices until fragrant, about 3 minutes or so.

Lower the heat to medium and add the garlic, ginger, and onions. Saute, stirring regularly until the onions are caramelized, about 20 minutes.

Next add the rest of the water, the potatoes, cauliflower and maple syrup. Cover and cook 20 minutes until tender. Once tender, remove the lid off the pan to let any extra water evaporate.

Lastly squeeze half a lemon over the top. Garnish with cilantro or chopped scallions.

Serve over rice.

PIZZA

SERVINGS
2-4

PREP TIME
20 MINUTES

COOK TIME
30 MINUTES

CRUST INGREDIENTS

2 1/2	cups flour	
1	tsp sugar	
2	tsp salt	
2	tbsp water	
1	package (.25oz) active dry yeast	
1	cup warm water	

SAUCE INGREDIENTS

1	medium tomato
1/4	cup sun-dried tomatoes, soaked
1/4	tsp each cayenne& salt
~	small handful of fresh basil
1	garlic clove
4	tbsp nutritional yeast
2	tbsp hemp seeds
1/4	cup water

TOPPINGS

Sliced red onion, baby broccoli, eggplant, mushrooms, sun-dried tomato, corn

INSTRUCTIONS

Preheat oven to 450°F. In a medium bowl, dissolve yeast and sugar in warm water. Let stand until creamy, about 10 minutes.

Stir in flour and salt. Using a whisk beat until smooth. Let rest for 5 minutes.

Turn dough out onto a lightly floured surface and pat or roll into a round ball. Roll it out into the size, shape and thickness you want. Transfer crust to a pizza pan.

Take your sauce ingredients and blend on low in your blender until smooth. The sauce should be thick so add the water in slowly.

Add on the sauce and all toppings and bake in oven for 15-20 minutes. Let cool for 5 minutes before serving.

At the very end we shredded one cashew on a microplane to make it look like parmesan and added dried basil and red pepper flakes over the top.

STUFFED CABBAGE ROLLS

MAKES	PREP TIME	COOK TIME
4-6 ROLLS	10 MINUTES	90 MINUTES

ROLLS

1   head of cabbage - 10 leaves

1   jar pasta sauce

Take your head of cabbage and place in a large pot of water and boil for a few minutes to soften. You want to be able to gently peel away the leaves. We will only be using the biggest leaves from the outside of the cabbage for this recipe.

STUFFING

2   cups red lentils, rinsed & drained

4   cups water

1/2   onion, minced

3   garlic cloves, minced

1   carrot, shredded

1   stalk celery, minced

2   cups bread crumbs

2   tbsp ground flax + 2 tbsp warm water

2   tbsp tamari or soy sauce

1   tsp each of garlic powder, oregano, basil, paprika, chili powder

1   cup jasmine rice, uncooked

INSTRUCTIONS

First combine the ground flax with the 2 tbsp of warm water so that it can sit and turn into jelly. Next put the lentils and water in a large pot, bring to a boil, reduce heat to simmer and let cool until the water is absorbed, about 20 minutes.

While the lentils are cooking take the onion, garlic, celery and carrot and simmer in about 1/4 cup of water until slightly cooked. Next add in the soy sauce and seasonings and stir to combine. When the lentils are finished cooking, place them in a food processor, add in the onion, garlic, celery and carrot mix and process until combined. Next add in your flax seed mix and slowly add in the bread crumbs, 1/4 cup at a time, processing in between.

Once all is combined place in a large mixing bowl and combine with the jasmine rice. Scoop mixture into cabbage leaves, add a dollop of sauce on top of each one and roll lengthwise. Tucking the ends under as you go, you can secure them with a toothpick if you wish, remove before serving.

Place the rolls in a large baking dish and cover with sauce. Bake at 350°F for one hour until the cabbage leaves are translucent and the inside is hot. Enjoy!

TARKA DAHL

SERVINGS	PREP TIME	COOK TIME
4-6	10 MINUTES	30 MINUTES

INGREDIENTS

2 cups red lentils, rinsed & drained

4 cups water + 1/4 cup water

2 tsp tumeric powder

2 tsp cumin seeds

1 small onion, minced

3 garlic cloves, minced

1/2 tsp cayenne

1 tsp garam masala

1 tsp coriander, ground

1 tsp fresh ginger, minced

1 15 oz can diced tomatoes, drained

1/2 cup frozen spinach

INSTRUCTIONS

Place the lentils and water in a sauce pan and bring to a boil. Reduce heat to simmer and stir in the turmeric. Let this cook 20 minutes while we get everything else ready.

Using a small pan over medium heat lightly toast the cumin seeds for a few minutes. Once toasted set aside.

Add the 1/4 cup water to a sauce pan over medium heat, add in the garlic, ginger, onions and sauté until translucent. Add in your cumin seeds, tomatoes, and the rest of your spices.

Now the lentils should be completely softened and absorbed into the water, combine with the rest of ingredients and lastly stir in your frozen spinach.

Serve over rice and add a tiny bit of salt to the top of your bowl if you wish.

THAI VEGETABLE SOUP

SERVINGS
4

PREP TIME
5 MINUTES

COOK TIME
20 MINUTES

INGREDIENTS

6   cups vegetable broth
1   onion, chopped
4   garlic cloves, minced
4   oz rice noodles
2   tbsp tamari
3   Thai chili peppers
2   tbsp fresh lemon grass, chopped
1/4   cup ginger root, chopped
1   handful of mushrooms
1/2   cup carrots, shredded
1   small zucchini, diced
1/4   cup bamboo shoots
1   handful bok choy, sliced
~   any other veggies you like

INSTRUCTIONS

Fill one medium pot half way with water and bring to a boil.

Add in your rice noodles and cook until ready about 10-12 minutes depending on the thickness of your noodles. Drain and rinse with cold water. Set aside.

Add all the remaining ingredients to your pot and bring to a boil. Reduce heat to simmer and cook for ten minutes or until the vegetables are tender.

Pour into a large bowl, add in rice noodles and enjoy.

TORTILLA SOUP

SERVINGS
4

PREP TIME
5 MINUTES

COOK TIME
25 MINUTES

INGREDIENTS

2   lbs frozen organic white corn
2   garlic cloves, minced
2   bsp white onion, minced
1   jalapeño, deseeded & minced
1 1/2   lbs plum tomatoes, diced
1   tbsp cumin
1   tsp salt
1/2   tsp chili powder
1   tsp cayenne
1   quart vegetable stock
~   garnish with avocado

INSTRUCTIONS

Add 1 lb of corn and all the rest of the ingredients to a medium saucepan and bring to a boil. Reduce heat to low and let cook for 5-10 minutes until fragrant.

Ladle the soup into your blender and blend on high until smooth.

Return back to sauce pan add the rest of the corn and cook on low another 10 minutes until reheated.

Add some avocado or cilantro to the top and enjoy :)

SPRING ROLLS

MAKES	PREP TIME	COOK TIME
8 ROLLS	10 MINUTES	10 MINUTES

ROLL INGREDIENTS

1	head iceberg lettuce, shredded
2	cups carrots, shredded
1	bunch cilantro, minced
2	oz vermicelli rice noodles
8	rice paper sheets

SAUCE INGREDIENTS

1/4	cup creamy peanut butter
2	tbsp unseasoned rice vinegar
1	tbsp lime juice
1	tbsp tamari
3	tbsp maple syrup
2	garlic cloves, minced
1	tsp ginger, minced
1	tsp salt
1/4	tsp red pepper flakes

INSTRUCTIONS

For the rolls, toss all the salad ingredients in a large mixing bowl. Prepare your rice vermicelli according to the package. Usually they only need to be placed in hot water for 10-15 minutes. Make sure after they are done cooking to rinse them with cool water to stop the cooking process.

Once rinsed, drain them and let them dry a bit in a colander. To use the rice paper you will need to either dunk it in a large bin of water or what I like to do is lightly run them under water as I use them.

To get started get one rice paper roll wet and let it sit on the counter until it has become a bit tacky (1 minute or so). When the paper is ready we will take about 1/8 of the noodles and 1/8 of the lettuce mixture and place it inside the center of the roll. Then roll the rice paper tightly around folding the edges up as you go. Repeat this process until all the filling is gone. It will make about 8 rolls depending on the size of your rice paper.

For the dressing, blend all the ingredients on high until smooth and serve on the side.

VEGGIE STEW

SERVINGS	PREP TIME	CROCKPOT TIME
4	10 MINUTES	3-4 HOURS

INGREDIENTS

2	lbs red potatoes, chopped
1	small rutabaga, chopped
1	white onion, chopped
5	medium carrots, chopped
1	1lb bag frozen peas
1	1/2 cups red lentils, rinsed
4	garlic cloves, minced
~	salt & pepper to taste

INSTRUCTIONS

This is another super easy crockpot meal.

First peel and roughly chop your potatoes, rutabaga, onion and carrots and throw into the crockpot. Next add in your lentils, and garlic. Then add in your quart of veggie stock and set on low for 3-4 hours.

This one doesn't take long to cook, so it's a great meal for a lazy Sunday.

Right before serving add in the frozen peas and mix until they are incorporated.

Season with salt and pepper if you wish.

RAW SPICY CORN SOUP

SERVINGS	PREP TIME	COOK TIME
1-2	10 MINUTES	0 MINUTES

JUICE INGREDIENTS

4	roma tomatoes
2	carrots
4	stalks of celery
1	medium zucchini
2	cups of greens of your choice

BLENDER INGREDIENTS

1	lb raw corn
2	garlic cloves
1	tbsp cumin
1	tsp chili powder
1/2	tsp cayenne

BASE INGREDIENTS

1	lb raw corn
1/2	avacado
2	tbsp cilantro, chopped
1/4	tsp salt (optional)

INSTRUCTIONS

First process all your juice ingredients through a juicer. If you don't have a juicer, there are instructions in the information section to juice fruits and vegetables using a nut milk bag.

Add the juice to the blender and blend on high with the spices, garlic and 1 lb of corn until smooth.

Separate remaining 1 lb of corn into two serving bowls and pour the soup mixture over top.

Add cilantro and avocado on top and enjoy.

RAW PIZZA

SERVINGS 2	PREP TIME 30 MINUTES	DEHYDRATING TIME: 4-6 HOURS

CRUST INGREDIENTS

1	cup raw buckwheat groats
1/4	cup flax seeds
~	water

SAUCE INGREDIENTS

1/2	cup sun-dried tomatoes, soaked 3 hrs
2	Medjool dates
2-3	Roma tomatoes
1	tsp garlic powder
1	tsp onion powder

TOPPINGS

1	small zucchini, sliced & chopped
1/2	red & yellow pepper, diced
1/4	cup mushrooms, diced
1/4	cup red onion, diced
1/4	cup artichoke hearts, diced
2	tbsp olives, diced
1	handful fresh basil, chopped

INSTRUCTIONS

Place buckwheat groats and flax seeds in blender, process until a fine powder and place in big mixing bowl. Slowly add in water while mixing until you get a dough like consistency.

Spread out on parchment paper (I place between 2 pieces of paper and roll it out with a rolling pin) and place in dehydrator on 115 for 4-6 hours checking periodically.

Times will vary depending how thick you rolled out the dough. You want the crust to still have a little moisture. It should be slightly chewy just like a normal pizza crust when it's finished. Prepare raw marinara by adding the sun-dried tomato, dates and seasoning to your blender and add in the roma tomatoes one by one until you get a thick marinara-like consistency, it usually is about 2-3 roma tomatoes. Spread marinara all over the pizza crust and add toppings.

This pizza also tastes amazing the day after so if you don't finish it all it is great to take to work the next day and have as leftovers. Enjoy!

MEDITERRANEAN WRAP

SERVINGS	PREP TIME	COOK TIME
1	15 MINUTES	0 MINUTES

INGREDIENTS

1	large collard leaf
1/2	tomato, chopped
1/4	carrot, shredded
1	tbsp red onion, sliced
1	handful sprouts
1/2	avocado
1	serving Falafel (recipe in this book)

RAW HUMMUS

2	small zucchini, chopped
1/4	cup raw tahini
1/2	lime, juice of
1	garlic clove
1/4	tsp sea salt
1	tsp cumin
1	tsp cayenne (optional)

INSTRUCTIONS

To make your hummus we will combine all the ingredients in our blender and blend on high until smooth. This makes enough hummus for 4 wraps.

To assemble the wraps, take your collard leaf and place it face down. You want to cut as much of the stem out of the leaf by placing your knife horizontally to the leaf and sliding it down to the end. You may not be able to get all of the stem out but get it as close to the leaf as you can without ripping it. This makes it easier to roll.

Place all of your ingredients inside and top with hummus. This wrap is great without the falafels, I just always add them in because they give it a lot more volume.

Next we are going to roll this up like a burrito. Take the two sides of the wrap and fold them inward, then take the side of the wrap that is closest to you and fold over all the ingredients and roll.

Cut in half and serve with an extra side of hummus.

SWEET
TREATS

———————➤

LEMON SQUARE BARS

SERVINGS
6

PREP TIME
15 MINUTES

CHILL TIME
2-3 HOURS

INGREDIENTS

20	Medjool dates, pitted
2	cups mulberries
2	cups dried figs or apricots
1/4	cup coconut flakes
~	zest from 1 lemon

INSTRUCTIONS

These lemon squares are great to have for breakfast and excellent to bring to work or school for a snack.

Combine all the ingredients in a food processor and process until it is well combined.

Push the mixture into a glass pan to form in place. Then place the pan into the refrigerator for a few hours until firm.

Cut into pieces and serve. Keep this in the fridge or freezer so it stays fresh to eat all week long.

RAW CHOCO CHIP COOKIES

MAKES	PREP TIME	CHILL TIME
6-8 COOKIES	20 MINUTES	2-3 HOURS

INGREDIENTS

15	Medjool dates, pitted
1/4	cup water
2	cups raw oats
1/4 c	up coconut flakes
2	tbsp cacao nibs
1	tsp vanilla
~	pinch of salt (optional)

INSTRUCTIONS

In your food processor, combine the oats, dates, coconut flakes, vanilla, salt and cacao nibs and process for a minute or so.

Next slowly add in the water until a dough like consistency forms. Take the mixture out and form into small balls, place these on a piece of parchment paper.

Press the balls into a cookie shape and place in the refrigerator for 1-2 hours so they can firm up.

Keep them stored in the refrigerator when you are not devouring them for freshness. Enjoy :).

GRANOLA

SERVINGS	PREP TIME	COOK TIME
6	10 MINUTES	0 MINUTES

INGREDIENTS

1/2	cup rolled oats
10	Medjool dates, pitted
1/2	cup mulberries
1/4	cup shredded coconut
2-3	tbsp cacao nibs

INSTRUCTIONS

Place all your ingredients in your food processor and process until you reach a granola like consistency.

I use a cheap food processor and process for about a minute. It will vary depending on if you are using a blender or food processor. If you are using a Vitamix only pulse this 4-5 times as you don't want it to blend.

This will last a while if you store it in the fridge in a glass, airtight container.

Use the granola to top your smoothie bowls, coconut yogurt or banana ice-cream.

RAW DONUT HOLES

| MAKES 12 DONUT HOLES | PREP TIME 20 MINUTES | DEHYDRATING TIME: 30 MINUTES |

INGREDIENTS

2	bananas
20	Medjool dates, pitted (soaked 2 hours)
1/4	cup water
1	tsp cinnamon
2	cups raw oats
1/4	cup shredded coconut

INSTRUCTIONS

First, soak your dates for 2 hours. Take your oats and place in blender or food processor. Process on high until you get a flour like consistency. Transfer oat flour to a large mixing bowl and set aside.

Next take your bananas, dates, water, and cinnamon and place in your blender. Blend on high until you get a smoothie like consistency. Pour this mixture into your oat flour and mix well until there are no dry spots left.

Next we are going to be placing these on parchment paper and into the dehydrator. The mixture is still pretty wet so you want to either use a ice cream scoop or a spoon and divide these up into 10 small mounds that are separated from each other. Use up all the batter. Place in dehydrator on 115°F for about 3 hours. We don't want these to become incredibly dry or hard, we just want to be able to roll them into a ball.

Once they have been dehydrating take the tray out of the dehydrator and one by one, take the mounds of batter and roll them into small donut hole shaped balls. Once you get them in the right form, roll them into shredded coconut and set aside. Do this until they are all done. Store in an airtight container in the fridge to maintain freshness.

MINT CHOCOLATE CHIP NICE CREAM

SERVINGS	PREP TIME	COOK TIME
1	10 MINUTES	0 MINUTES

INGREDIENTS

4	frozen bananas
1	tsp of barley grass powder or any green powder
1	drop of peppermint oil or 1 handful of fresh mint
1	tbsp carob or cacao powder
1	tbsp cacao nibs
~	extra cacao nibs or coconut flakes

INSTRUCTIONS

In a high speed blender, blend all ingredients on low using the tamper to push everything back towards the blade and slowly increase the speed of the blender until everything is nice and smooth.

If you don't have a high quality blender with a tamper, take the frozen bananas out of the freezer and let them thaw at room temperature for atleast 30 minutes.

If the blender spins out, turn off the blender and push the frozen banana mixture towards the blade with a spatula or spoon and blend again. You may have to do this a number of times but if you don't add in water, you'll get a very thick banana nice cream.

Top with extra cacao nibs or coconut flakes and pile in a small mason jar, take a photo so you can boggle your friend's minds on instagram with the height of your nice cream ;)

RAW HEALTHY CINNAMON ROLLS

MAKES
6-8 ROLLS

PREP TIME
20 MINUTES

DEHYDRATING
TIME 12 HOURS

INGREDIENTS

2	cups oats
1/4	cup water
20	dates, pitted
2	ripe bananas
1/4	tsp cardamom
1/4	tsp nutmeg
1/2	tsp vanilla
1/4	tsp salt (optional)

FILLING

20	dates, pitted
1	tbsp cinnamon
2	tbsp water
1	tbsp raisins for topping

INSTRUCTIONS

Start by placing the oats in a blender and blending for a few seconds until they turn to a flour. Transfer to a large mixing bowl. In the blender add in fresh dates (if you are using dried dates make sure to soak them a few hours before hand), water, the bananas, spices and blend until everything is well incorporated. Dump this mixture into the flour mix and blend well into a dough.

Place this dough mixture between 2 sheets of parchment paper and roll out with a rolling pin into a large flat rectangle. Place in dehydrator on 115 for 8 or so hours until you can remove the top parchment paper sheet without the dough sticking to it. Continue to dehydrate for another 4-6 more, until the dough is no longer sticky and is rollable.

Add all ingredients for the cinnamon filling into your blender and blend until smooth.

Spread the filling over the dough and roll it up into a long thin cylinder. Slice into pieces and top with raisins and cinnamon.

CONTINUED LEARNING

LEAN & CLEAN EBOOK

14 day meal plan for
maximum weight loss

highcarb.co/lean

WEIGHT LOSS CHEAT SHEET

30 recipes + tons of info
to get you started!

highcarb.co/cheatsheet

INSTANT POT EBOOK

30 simple oil-free vegan
pressure cooker recipes.

highcarb.co/epic

PLANT APP

100s of recipes and customizable
meal plans right in your pocket.

highcarb.co/app

Made in the USA
Monee, IL
22 August 2021